COME OCTOBER

BY

DAMIEN ARK

FERAL DOVE BOOKS

SEATTLE
1998 DODGE RAM VAN
BANGOR, ME

2023

FAGGOT

CHILD

Fourth-grade gym class. For the first five minutes, we're allowed to talk freely before doing stretches and then shift to our routine activities. That means I'd have a moment to sit around and watch everyone else standing up and conversing while anxiously twiddling my fingers in my lap. Once free time is over, I finally stand up, and then big bully Brice comes up to me and thrusts a thumb into my chest.

"Hey, you know what GAP stands for, right?" He continues to nudge at my gray GAP hoodie. "It means that you're gay and proud. GAP. Get it, faggot? You're a gaywad! Haha, ha ha ha."

His thumb manifests into a fist that pummels into my stomach. I grip the pain and cough violently as the air is knocked right out of my little fragile angel body while I'm also hoping nobody just witnessed that. Thank G-d that nobody did.

When I get home, I yank all of my GAP clothes out of my closet, toss them against the plastic Crayola-red racecar mattress my dad picked out for me when we moved here, and then I tell mom how I want to dress from now on. I want to look like Brice. Make me look like the other boys on my baseball team: no more stripes, polos, polka-dots, or baggy blue pants. But we're poor, so it takes some time. She sells most of it, and then I get all the trendy clothes that match what the other cool kids have. I'm standing in front of the mirror in my room, the young Anakin Skywalker poster to its left, and I check myself out. Basketball shorts, calf-high black socks with two white stripes at the top, Converse shoes, Pink Floyd T-Shirt with the Dark Side of the Moon album cover on it, bought from Target.

"Mom. What's a faggot?"

She tells me about my gay uncle and gay first cousin, how I shouldn't use that word, and how daddy hates them, but she thinks they're the friendliest people she knows. They're men that like men.

"Like Riley?"

Two words like an avalanche like the tornado that hit mom's house when she was a little girl like the unintended pregnancy at age seventeen like teen homelessness like snorting blow and jumping off your high school rooftop like letting a close friend watch over your son like when your son walks in to find you sobbing on a toilet seat but you're not pooping so he asks what's wrong like when you see your son holding a kitchen knife under the computer table like finding out that you're a faggot forever, just like him, and you're not sure you'll ever find out what that means.

X   X   X

Mom loves to watch Oprah, but I don't get it because she cries most of the time that it's on. I sit across from her on the sofa with my feet on her lap. Sometimes she squeezes my toes, which is how I can tell she's frustrated. Oprah a talks about an army somewhere in the middle of Africa that kills all men in the villages and then rapes the women. They remove the women's clitorises with a razor and pluck their pubic hairs and murder the rest of the family in front of them before raping them. She pauses the television when she notices me staring through her. Not too long after that, I snap out of it, and she sees into me. She sees it but says nothing.

X   X   X

*Riley's favorite band was The Cure and Disintegration was his
favorite album. Listening to their music used to trigger me, but
now I imagine hearing what he heard when I listen to them.
My mom listened to Nine Inch Nails. I stole her copy of The
Downward Spiral in third or fourth grade and played it almost
every day. Now I can't listen to it anymore, as it reminds me of
her. Strange how trauma and years of brainwashing have told
me who deserves to be forgiven and who should be hated.*

*It's easier to imagine that he was a vampire. That what he did
was crucial for his survival. It's like that because he knew how
to make me see him as a victim and not something entirely evil.
So when I think about him, I imagine he planted teeth marks
across my neck. That's why I fell for it, kept my mouth shut,
and obeyed him like a mindless doll.*

X   X   X

Riley picks me up from school and takes me back to
his apartment. There's a time when he's not living
with us anymore. I see him less and go over to my
friend J's house more often, sometimes multiple times
a week, since my parents are rarely home, and then
I'm also put in an afterschool daycare. This makes him
sick with rage, vengeful over my parents for kicking
him out because he wasn't making housing payments.
What started as our playful little secret becomes
something that has him sobbing afterward and then
lashing out at me.

His apartment is infested with scorpions. My eyes constantly stare at the floor while we're playing a Mortal Kombat video game in the dark, and I swear that I see them sometimes, but then I forget that it's what's next to me that's causing the sudden jumps in fear, not the bugs that only come out when we're asleep. After Riley kills me in the video game, he uses a cheat code to rip my spinal cord out of my body and beat my corpse with it. For a moment, I feel something crawling on my heel, so I kick myself off the couch, imagining that it must have been a scorpion.

"You said you wouldn't run off again," Riley raises his voice. "You fucking liar! I'll fucking kill you!"

He twists me around, holds onto one of my shoulders, and punches me in the nose. There was a crunch, but I wasn't sure if the bone had been broken. I try to scream, but my body won't let me. All I can do is sob while cupping my face as blood drools to my chin. Then it's, "Stop fucking crying!" But I can't, so he yanks my hair and bashes my forehead against the coffee table. When I fall to the carpet, he pulls down my white basketball shorts and underwear and throws himself on top of me, cupping the weight of his hands and arms all around my stomach and chest. His canine teeth peck into my neck to draw blood. Then it's, "I said I love you." When we kiss, it's like mommy and daddy, and it's okay now, this is sex, it hurts, but it's love, you love me, it's love.

X   X   X

The hospital I was born inside of is now a slaughterhouse with a pool of blood near one side of it. You can smell the disembow-eled cattle day and night throughout the small Midwest town. The people that live there are either in poverty and on meth or have a million-dollar house hidden behind massive hills of sweet corn. The synagogue once there became a church not too long after my birth. With that, the small Jewish population left it all behind. You can smell the corpses from miles away. The scent reminds me of my childhood, my ancestors, and everything related to me, and all I see is soaked in blood, waiting to be sucked into the bone-shredding machines and molded to gelatin. My great-grandmother might have escaped Hitler, but I'm sure I'll have my brains blown out for being a faggot and a Jew soon enough, and most of my family massacred later on.

X   X   X

My friends probably thought of it as experimenting, but I knew what I was doing and the pleasure I was getting from it. I'd spend almost every day being a hypersexed kid that sought to play with as many dicks as possible. If I were home alone, in that blinding white vessel of a house, I'd toss myself around in boredom, humping my pillow and bedframe, and spend hours jacking off. Thanks to Riley, I knew how to access porn and clear my browser history. Sex. Skin. Boys. Men. The vampiric curse was festering in my blood.

There was a boy at daycare that I fell for, who physically looked like big bully Brice, but befriended me. He had light brown hair gelled up and a darker tan than me, a sparrow's face filled with intriguing confidence. Evan was intelligent, obsessed with astronomy, and drew detailed pictures of futuristic spaceships and planets he read about on Wikipedia. Of my five friends at daycare, he was the most into 'experimenting.'

Here was our vanishing act. We would sneak off to the restrooms during recess, which was hidden on one side and made it difficult for the staff to see where we went. The bathroom was compact, with flickering lights and sharp brick walls. When we stood across from each other, it was hard not to be already touching. Evan would pull his dick out first, which had a long teardrop foreskin, then I'd take out mine, much tinier and circumcised, and I'd rub it against his. We would stroke each other, sometimes even kiss, all of which I learned beforehand and taught him. \

My most vivid memory of him begins with my mouth on his cock, giving him his first blowjob while he held all my clothes in a ball against his chest. One of the staff must have caught onto us. Just as I could tell he was close to his dry cum, the fat cunt started beating on the door and called out Evan's name. He told her to hold on as we dressed quickly, then he flushed the toilet, ran water in the sink, opened it way too far, and let her catch a glimpse of me in there with him.

"D was trying to help me find my friendship bracelet," Evan lied. "Found it, though."

She saw through the lie and taunted that she knew what we did because other boys had done it before and that it was an unforgivable sin that could send us to hell. She swore that she'd tell our parents if she ever saw us doing it again.

We met later that day at the playground. He was sitting on the tar floor, picking at it with one hand, holding the rainbow friendship bracelet I made for him in his other hand. I didn't understand the problem, so I imagined we'd be more careful next time.

"If my parents find out we did that…" he stuttered, the fear of hell and his parents cemented in his head. "We can't hang out anymore. I'm sorry."

After elementary school, I saw him again in my first year of high school. He remembered everything we had done together. I shared English class with him, and as I walked into the classroom on the first day and passed his desk, he knocked the books out of my hand and cursed, "Watch yourself, faggot."

Seeing how vital it was for him to show off how repressed he was, I knew that he was just like me.

Another faggot child hiding behind a mask and begging to be torn out from this world. And with that vampire blood inside of me, all I could imagine was what it would be like to see him dead.

X   X   X

Summer of 2004, June 13, I'm ten years old, and this is the year that I lose all aspects of myself that made me seem like a boy, a child, while never maturing into a teenager or a man. By the end of that summer and after I've completed 5th grade, the teeth marks given to me by Riley will have transformed me into something so ugly and inhuman that my sole purpose in existing will be to try and kill myself every day.

It's Texas and gay marriage is illegal. Every word is gay and queer and fag and faggot. The second you realize that you're one of those words, you create your cocoon and do anything possible to seem straight, no matter how much it destroys you. The slurs are casually uttered in every hallway, classroom, home, playground, locker room, and in a solitary bedroom.

I lower my prepubescent voice as much as possible and sit with dad and my uncles while watching X-Files, 80s slasher movies, and splatter porn like Hostel and the Saw series. Violence makes you a man. And yet, I'm still gay. My cock still gets excited for other boys and men. And then I envision jaws being torn off and cannibalistic monsters and little aliens and ten-foot-tall Cylons and twinks online jacking off in the shower, uncut cocks, like Evan's, who I'll never stroke or suck off or kiss again.

X   X   X

Daycare wasn't the same as it was in 4th grade. I'd already done all the activities of going to shitty Disney movies, waterparks, skating rinks, and museums. Even Medieval Times bored me now.

During the summer, I was stuck in daycare from six-thirty in the morning to seven every night and always the last kid to go home. The staff would pick fights with my mom since they had to do overtime to watch over me. When I could leave early, be with J on weekdays, or have baseball practice or games, those were the days that brought me joy. Otherwise, I'd rotate from the computer lab to the arcade room to the art room to recess in a constant state of depressive boredom.

Evan wasn't at daycare anymore. It made me wonder if he had confessed his guilt and told his parents. After all, he did wear that cross necklace with pride. During recess, I'd sit on the grassy hill behind the monolithic playground that probably cost tens of thousands of dollars to build. My pale face would be drenched in sweat as I'd stare down at the kids playing basketball and in line for the tetherball tournament. I'd focus on that compact path between the tall wooden fence and the daycare building's wall, leading to the bathrooms where we had played with each other's dicks. I craved to do it with him again, just one more time, but all I could do was chew on blades of grass, pretend to be as cool as him, and replay what he said to me in the same spot where we sat a year ago.

At the age of ten, I became a blooming flower of perversion, unable to recognize its scent of hatred and rot. Most of my thoughts were of sex. Penises, blowjobs, being penetrated, what it might be like to penetrate others, kissing, licking all over. I wanted to sink my teeth into others, just like what had been done to me. Riley was gone for good, yet the sterile void of emotions I had for him was unconsciously magnifying.

X   X   X

My mother worked in malls across the metroplex, managing various stores, from Victoria's Secret to Coach to selling expensive furniture. Behind each department store was the backroom where all items were kept, along with my mother's office. Behind that door were hallways like tentacles that led to other storerooms and inevitably to places like the dumpster, stairways, the rooftop, and the security room. Not all malls had cameras inside the tentacles of their hidden white cavities.

There were times when my parents couldn't afford daycare bills. Dad couldn't take me to work, so I'd often have to come with mom to the mall. Usually, that meant staring at handbags, women's lingerie, and kids' clothes, sorting clothes for her, and following the other employees around, getting a few dollars from them so I could roam freely and have solitary fun on my own.

Sometimes, Mom would catch me in Hot Topic on her lunch break, and then she'd buy some CDs for herself. Shitty post-grunge and alternative rock that everyone else enjoyed. Other times, I'd go ice skating. Eventually, other retail workers knew me by name, letting me come by as much as I wanted for free.

I'd often spend hours staring at the NorthPark Mall's art sculptures. Sometimes, I'd even talk to famous artists that had their art showcased at the mall. Momma, can we live in this building? I love the architecture here. Can I stay here forever? I don't want to go back to daycare. It's boring, and I don't even have real friends there. Everyone hates me. Do you even love me? I don't want to go to school. I'd do homework in the cafeteria while eating greasy Chinese food. One of your coworkers tells me about the life of Fela Kuti, and then we go ice skating together. I grow closer to her and the other coworkers than to you or dad. You're both so busy, working like psychotic machines, unable to see that the damage is festering and on the verge of becoming unrepairable.

X   X   X

Grandma visits. Dad picks me up from the mall, I'm in the backseat, and grandma's in the passenger. She asks me if I believe in angels. It's a fucking shame you're raising him as a Jew, you know. We Catholics. Mom, I don't even believe in G-d. And you let them fucking win this shit? Okay, D, do you believe in angels? Oh, I don't know. I've never seen one before. So I don't think so. See? See? This is what happens when you raise a kid with a Jew and an Atheist. I'll take him to Church and show him. Show him what? You're not taking him to fucking shit. Mom, if you don't shut the fucking hell up, I'll slam on the fucking--. See, you're scaring him. He doesn't even know what the fucking Holocaust is yet. If you ever say any of this stupid fucking religious shit to my son after today, I'll make sure you never see him again.

One of mom's biggest pet peeves in the mall is Christmas music, which starts as soon as Halloween ends. Mom doesn't even believe in G-d, but she still took me to Shabbat services; she wanted me to be a good Jew and hoped to please the Jewish side of my family. It didn't matter if I paid attention or learned Hebrew; I just had to prove to the others that I went.

It feels like I'm constantly being indoctrinated. At least you can wear a yarmulke. Wait, no, don't do that. You'll get bullied and called a faggot and a kike, especially with your lisp. If I wore a Star of David at work, I might not get as good ratings or promotions. I don't even believe in any of the G-d shit, anyway, so fuck it.

X   X   X

I was at daycare that day when someone jumped down four stories from the high-rise at the mall and landed right into the skating rink, *ka-splat,* dead as fuck. The mall went into a blackout. Mom was probably thinking of when she tried to jump off her high school rooftop in eleventh or twelfth grade, not too long before she got pregnant with me. What had led to it? Something about being depressed while on a coke binge, probably not wanting to go with my parents on another pipelining trip to the middle of nowhere in the Midwest.

There's a jar of sand on Mom's desk that I made at daycare for Mother's Day. I don't know what colors are in it, though, because I'm colorblind. She's never at her office because she's busy trying to win all of those awards so that she doesn't have to have me here and can afford to put me back in daycare and baseball practice, maybe get me some new clothes that I'd like, not the tacky shit I'd get bullied over.

Sorry for not seeing how hard you had been working just to give me a chance and how much you wanted to protect me, but it was impossible. There are so many rapists in this world, but you know that better than I do.

First life memory. Ironically, my favorite mall my mother worked at was where I was first molested— the one with all the million-dollar sculptures. Us in roach-infested subsidized housing. Yelling, fuck this shitty ass job, fuck retail, I'll never dress like a clown and sell children's clothes ever again, I'll sell women's lingerie from now on. Don't fucking tell me what I have to do when you're still in school, and I'm making more than you.

Hiding under the computer desk in the office with a kitchen knife, Dad finds me and asks me what I'm doing. I thought he was going to kill mommy. I give him the blade, and he embraces me with a genuine hug, confessing that he's trying to do better for me, mom too, and then I go back to the PC to play Backyard Baseball.

Still, shit, it could be a lot fucking worse, like losing your five-year-old child in the bathroom mall when he goes for a pee. A couple of hours later, he's amnesiac, completely dressed, but his underwear is missing, hidden in the tentacles of the mall's white cavities, with no evidence to be traced back to the perpetrator. Then you say fuck it, let him keep roaming these malls; now he's got thick skin.

When the stores had to be renovated every few months, mom worked eighty hours a week and sometimes slept on the storage room's hardwood floor. On the way home, she'd vomit in the backseat, sob manically, and beat her head against the car's wheel while The Downward Spiral by Nine Inch Nails would play on full blast.

I'd do sleepovers at one of her work friend's high-rise apartments in Fort Worth. I'd slip out of the bottom part of his bunk bed, get dressed, and we'd talk about shit like rigging the Dave and Buster's Machines, Lego sets that just came out at the new Lego store, going ice-skating, that crazy suicide, let's touch dicks again sometime, can I borrow your mom's Tool CD collection, Dragon Ball Z reruns on Toonami. I can recall how I'd imagine his bedroom window was above cotton clouds while we'd cuddle together and watch Robin Hood, The Jungle Book, all on VHS.

I was lost in the mall's hallways, dressed in my Halloween skeleton costume and wearing ice-skating shoes. The dumpster smells worse than the farms back home in Iowa. Hot Dallas shitbags were spewing into the dumpster. A young man working as a dishwasher for the Cheesecake Factory gave me a snack by that dumpster. He asked if he could kiss me on my cheek. I squeezed the plastic heart in my right hand filled with red dye and took off the mask for him. He pecked his lips on mine, and then I skated off, hands rattling, my heart like a timebomb, and I couldn't explain why, but when I made it to the skating rink, all I could do was sit there and watch the others while painfully twisting the head of my cock with two fingers.

D lived with his best friend for a few months. He was almost adopted until his parents finally got their shit figured out to the best of their abilities. Being with him in that haunted hundred-and-twenty-year-old Victorian mansion or at daycare were the only moments that brought him solace. They'd drink root beer and play GameCube games until they passed out with controllers still in their hands. On other days, they'd fall asleep in the same bed, burrowed together, after hours of playing Roller Coaster Tycoon 2 and filming stop motion animation films with Legos and clay figurines.

If I could live in the sound of the PS2 starting up for a million years, if I could play baseball as good as the kids on Backyard Baseball, do you remember always getting pissed off while playing Super Monkey Ball on GameCube, killing everyone on Grand Theft Auto: Vice City but we had to keep the volume low so your parents wouldn't wake up and notice how violent the game was, the hours upon hours of mastering SSX 3, trading notebooks of codes for bosses and other objects we were making in ZZT, eating Hot Cheetos in the same sleeping bag while our Game Boy's clamored as if to become one, lost in the belly of Metroid Fusion, excising my nightmares. Farewell because this world cannot be my permanent reality. G'night, J.

When D and J couldn't hang out on the weekdays, they'd play online games and pretend to be teenage hackers on message boards. At daycare, J would bring floppy disks with him so they could manifest their DOS ZZT games both at home and in the computer lab. Other kids would compete in beating the games they made. In the arcade room, the two were always glued shoulder to shoulder near the front door where the R-Type arcade cabinet stood tall over their heads.

The game was nearly impossible to beat, like how in their own DOS games using a cheat code would immediately cause a GAME OVER. Then at four-thirty in the afternoon, J would leave, and by five-thirty, almost all of the kids were gone, leaving D alone on a carpet that he would roll on in boredom without being bothered. How a boy should never feel that alone in the world. GAME OVER.

We are in each other's spit and blood. We've shared off the same plate, slept under the same sheets, you've seen the vampire in my eyes, and I've seen the ghost in yours. You have seen me die countless times. When I'm nonexistent to others, I am you. When you're lost to the world, I am you. For this brief moment of a few more weeks, before I'm handed back to my mother and father, we can prove that ghosts exist in your vermillion Victorian home. We can leave the camcorder on all night to come back later and see if there's any presence of the spirit that's been haunting us. We are idiots and geniuses designing websites with Claymation videos while we chug liters of soda at midnight and play Windwaker and Majora's Mask. The longer we embrace it, the more we can feel like children forever.

They weren't on the same team, but they both played baseball. D fucking hated it, while J remained indifferent but always calm and careless about it and everything else in his life with this barely audible voice. Sometimes, they'd go to the skating rink and kill time at the batting practice nets outside of it. Early 2000s R&B blasted through the doors as the sun melted through a polluted starless sky. They could see children skating through a window while Ed Edd n' Eddy played on a massive projector screen. Sports made D feel less like a fag to his parents. At age seven, he got hit in the face by a soccer ball and swore he'd never play sports again. But then he said fuck it and gave in because it wasn't just his parents or grandparents, but the kids at daycare too, that kept seeing him as a nerdy loser faggot. Even after swinging a bat and putting on the helmet, he found out that it wouldn't change anything; all the boys still called each other gaywads, queer, gay, fags, and faggots within every sentence of every conversation.

We'll be the first to unlock the true depths of the internet. My Myspace profile will have an emo Shadow from Sonic; I'll decorate him with monochromatic wings, a golden halo, wearing white Adidas drenched with moss, seashells superglued to them, glitter and ear piercings, and plastic beads over the soles. If I could live inside of the desolate Toonami spaceship and escape the fourth-grade classrooms, sitting with my legs crossed and my face glued to the ten-ton TV as I record Dragon Ball Z reruns on VHS tapes, if I could live far away with my internet friends on these forums, if I could delete myself as easily as clearing my history on Internet Explorer after watching gay porn on dad's computer, twisting my dick around as twinks piss on the faces of older men. Had I worn the dress, let him hook on the bra with the fake breasts, where would that have gone, would he have replaced Evan, or even Riley, would the trajectory change everything, or would it be another memory to relish, like picking at a bleeding sore in the gums? I could change the narrative, distort reality, I could cut open my wrist, string my neck, and make it my truth.

X   X   X

Everything is more haunting when you're a child. Everything is a skyscraper, ready to be unearthed, and wanting to sink its teeth into your fragile little bones. This was Dallas, after all. The concrete metropolis was like the malls was like the passages in J's house were like the long, unnerving daycare hallways D would get lost within.

4:30 PM. J would hear his name over the intercom. And then he'd go ghost. Walkie-talkies clicked and distorted words muttered out of them. Suddenly, D would find himself alone. Even though he was only a kid, he felt he could be that way forever, alone on the oversized playmat rug, with no friends to bond with, no soul naïve enough to fall in love with him. He'd focus on the staff member flicking off the lights to the art room, the arcade, and the lab, as they headed down the opaque hallway. All of the staff hated his mother more than him for being a faggot jew because they just wanted to get home, but her commute from work was two hours, meaning that she could only make it right around or after closing time.

He'd wait in the office for mommy and stare at his shoes while the daycare's owner would stare with embers in her eyes pinpointed on his skull. He didn't need to hear their voices to know they hated him. Ever since a staff member found him with another boy in a bathroom, he could feel their grunts and eyes on him and he knew why he was put in time-out more often than before. If he weren't looking at his shoes tapping together, he'd watch the security cameras on the TV behind her or read off the dates of the stack of VHS tapes on the right. He wondered if that specific day, when he and Evan entered the bathroom, was on video. Would it be held over his head until the day he died? When would they show it to his mom, and what would dad do? Would he be thrown off his favorite Dallas building, the glowing lime green one he always wanted to lick, kiss, and dry hump?

D pinched his underwear and wanted to cry. He wanted to pee so badly but wondered if the owner or the last staff member would remark if he asked to go the bathroom. Once he felt a single drop spill out, he finally asked if he could go, and they hesitantly let him through. After relieving himself, he stared down the hallway, a single tentacle, and gazed into an abyss, seemingly like a mortuary for children. Dusty curtains danced to the song of the wind and thunder, and the sky was a bath of lavender dreams. All of the windows were open, and he couldn't help but climb through one of them. There was a feeling in his chest, like the sting of a scorpion, and as he followed the sentiment, it led him back to the bathroom. When he opened the door, he felt the piercing of teeth through his skin and into his heart, cold invisible blood, but nothing seemed to be there. No, someone was definitely there. The vampire had taken the form of a spirit. He shut the door and whispered like the other kids did to scare one another, 'Bloody Mary, Bloody Mary, Bloody Mary....'

X   X   X

X   X   X

Feel the summer on your skin. Texas heat waves and endless droughts. Dead grass and boiling pool water. Chlorine, sweat, and powdered lemonade on your hands. We recorded our entire childhood on floppy disks and cassette tapes. The sound of towne lake. The sound of baseball cleats kicking through the mud. Singing country songs in the back of a pick-up truck. It was the sound of the wooden boards on the back porch creaking as we saw your mom watching Fox News and washing tomatoes from the garden in the kitchen. The days when you're not with your stepbrother, frenzied with boredom, sunbathing like a dying dog in your bedroom, waiting for the sun to set, to gleam rays of clementine over an unplugged transparent Sega Dreamcast. Days when we'd crawl on the floor, flicking glossy Yu-Gi-Oh cards across the room, bored of playing Pokemon Stadium for the thousandth time. You won't remember this, though.

X   X   X

Across the street from J's house were two brothers, nine and eleven years old, who D only met once. He never understood how his best friend knew them so well when he had never met them before. It's as if they existed only to be a half-buried memory in the gray matter of his brain. They seemed identical in looks, easy enough to be white blurs, faceless, ghost hair, smears in the humid air of tan skin.

The first thing he remembered about the brothers was the older one taking his hands and having him tie one of his mother's bras around his back. "Ma's got these fake boob thingies," the brother giggled. "Here. Feel them. Do you think they're like the real thing?" He stuffed them into the bra, danced in an oversized dress in front of D, and tongued lipstick. "Do you want to try?" The brother held his hands again, directed them to the bra, and squeezed his fingers tightly to simulate the grope of fake breasts. "Do you like that? You can take them and the dress off of me, and then I'll dress you."

Something about the feeling of a stranger's skin touching his made him think of tentacles of bathroom malls of vampire's teeth and being banged against a coffee table, so he blurted out, "I'm not a fucking queer, gaywad. What the fuck is wrong with you? You loser. You gross faggot."

Like Brice had done to him, he struck the older boy in the stomach and ran down the spiral staircase of the massive home. He didn't stop running until he reached the backyard pool's tip, tiny toes dangling over the edge, arms crossed with ire, eyes frozen in fear. His body shivered, and he thought of Iowa, where he was born, where his parents came from, his father as a child digging tunnels in the snow, his mom's house burning down, and then a tornado, baby universe, the spring rain over the cornfield seen from the sunroom as the family gathered around to play cards and drink and mourn.

J and the younger brother were doing laps in the pool. They teased D about not being able to swim. They wanted to teach him, but D was too afraid. Even though it calmed him to gaze at the fractals in the water, he couldn't help but feel that someday, what baptized others would drown him in his own hell. Un-expectedly, the older brother pantsed him nude and pushed him into the water with as much force as he could muster. D suddenly felt himself choking and thought, 'this is it, I'm going to die; it hurts so bad, and I can't find my way back up.' And there was a light melting above him like the Midwest snow he reached for, but when he passed through, nobody noticed or surrounded him in worry about what had happened. J and the two brothers had already forgotten and were splashing each other again. It wasn't until he was en-tirely out of the water that he realized he was naked and that his shorts and underwear were floating away from him. He'd gone ghost. GAME OVER.

X   X   X

You must remember this. I know you remember —

X   X   X

They faced the camcorder toward their bed, red light gleaming, a lamp on a dresser near the door, the door always shut, the taste of decay and dust, spirits all around them, visible and invisible. Because Texas is the most haunted state ever with the most vengeful undead clawing into the wooden bedframe, slicing its nails across your back while you're asleep and you're sweating through the sheets into an abyss, every graveyard a bad omen, a tombstone waiting to be licked (double-dog dare), it's in the bathroom, in the corner of your bedroom, and the only way to exorcise them is to leave the state behind. And J whispered in his ear as the raven-haired boy sat up on one arm, "I know it's a woman… And I think she might have been a maid or an enslaved person or a Native American or something. I was playing Pokemon in bed, and then she started banging on my keyboard. I woke up to find her hiding behind the curtain. The lower part of her body was all foggy and rotten. But the bathroom, that's where she hides the most. At the sink, in the bathtub…." Always wanting to hide behind the curtains. Bathrooms. D knew she was listening. It didn't matter how hard he squeezed his false brother's wrists in a panic, which he did throughout the night.

The piss anxiety. Always scared of bathrooms. Something about being lost in a mall. About the daycare bathroom. About what would come if he wouldn't ---. It always felt like a dream. Hallways like walking in a desert at night. He knew she was in there and waiting for him, and a part of him was afraid, but the other part wanted to see if he'd find her or someone different. J's bathroom was never renovated and still looked the same as when it was first constructed. There was a round white tub veiled with an equally pale shower curtain, which glowed from the moonlight, a chain that had to be pulled for his piss to flush, and a tall sink that required standing on a stool to operate. While he wiped his hands across his chest, he fell into a trance as he moved toward the bathtub. He knew what was hidden and didn't need to pull back the curtain, but did it anyway, and the eyes see nothing, but the skin feels all.

The footage went on until it took up too much memory. A few minutes before the boys woke up, they found her. She stood over their bed, gazing down at them, and swayed back into the sunlight. After supper, the video was mysteriously erased, and the keyboard was unplugged.

X   X   X

Angels and red orbs in the dust were to blame. It felt like someone was walking up the stairs with a camera. Like someone recorded us while we slept. That was, in a dream, I guess. J dreams that he lived in an abandoned church, and I dream that I was an anthropomorphic wolf playing with grasshoppers and minty green worms. When we woke up, we watched the tape of our dream. In who's memory?

X   X   X

GameCube and PlayStation 2 cheat codes memorized. My holographic Yu-Gi-Oh cards are across your bed. I'm trying to remember and repress everything at the same time. A Dallas Cowboys T-Shirt I wore despite hating the sport. Somersaults in the backyard, skating with gnarled bloody knees, your mother in the garden picking tomatoes, taking us to Bible lessons on Sunday, the first time I saw Jesus Christ bleeding out on a cross, my inability to understand why people wore the tool that their messiah was killed upon, and I could hear your heartbeat through the other earbud as we listened to German trance. Dare to tell your mother that heaven is to blame for everything. We could burn the Scholastic book fair down, draw cocks and galaxies on MS Paint and print a copy of it to pin above our computer monitors, blessed by data halos and trojan horses, customizable South Park avatars for Yahoo! Messenger and AOL, plastic plants soiled with dust on your grandmother's table at night, you'd watch her die, and I'd listen to the sound of my father's pacemaker ticking, our voice sped up like Chipmunks through the headphones on Audacity, how your mother caught a picture of a ghost on her Nokia flip-phone in monochrome, sex. There would be no need for a brother when he returned home the next day because he found something better in his left fist.

X   X   X

Bloody Mary idled like a statue behind D as he held himself up on the bathroom sink with his cock pressed against the front part. The sunlight beamed through stained glass windows and refracted onto him, which made his body throb and sweat. X was outside doing kickflips. D humped to the sound of cursing. "Fuck." Fucked it. "Shit." Harder. Until he gasped and felt his chest flatten into a void and found himself on a wet rug on the floor. It tasted like X, so he sucked on it and ate pieces of the soft shaggy carpet.

Downstairs. The long gyrating creek of a back door closed in slow motion. After D hurt himself enough times while J was upstairs playing Windwaker, he let the teenager bandage him while attempting to sit still in a rocking chair. The boy awkwardly looked him in the eyes briefly before he forced his vision on a cobweb and confessed, "I wanna be like you, someday. Really, I do."

"You wanna be like me," X repeated, eyes to the back of his head as he thought about it. "But you're already like me. You don't want to be me, trust me, but you're gonna be like me, anyway, because... I know what happened to you. So that's how it's gonna be. You'll be like me, and you'll hate everything, you'll probably end up on drugs, hurt yourself, like, you know, and if you don't know, it doesn't matter, because you will.

You look like I did when I was your age, so it fucks with me. It's scary. If I could go back to your age, I'd… I'd probably tell myself things aren't going to get better, and then I'd kill myself."

X shoved his skateboard under his left armpit, left D to think about what he said, the advice he had given him, and spent the rest of the evening smoking weed on the porch while he listened to shitty nu-metal.

TARANTULA

When I came out of the hallway, I found my parents squatting on the kitchen island and screaming like they'd seen the ugliest Medusa head on the ground. The fear in their eyes sunk into my chest cavity, and the tension elevated once I simultaneously heard them shout my name and saw what frightened them so badly. My feet kicked back, and I tripped as they do in horror movies, and then I lifted myself onto the counter, separated from my parents but free from the two massive brown recluse spiders. Dad had an irrational fear of spiders, despite being afraid of nothing else, while my mother was naturally disturbed by everything. I felt the fear consume me. The spiders were down there, but I imagined hundreds of them all over me. Eggs in my ears, behind my eyes, filling up my throat, vomiting a nest of venomous spiders out of my mouth and over my parents. Dad would sometimes jolt out of bed, yell as loud as he could, and still feel the spiders from his night terror crawling up his face or back. House of constant screaming underneath the ambiance of TV gunshots blaring. I felt my face bend and invert into a hexagon as I saw the venomous arachnid frozen in defensive mode. They were hellbent on killing us. I recalled when the three of us left the theater after seeing *The Lord of the Rings: The Return of the King* on opening night, how the moon had glimmered like a crimson rose, and on the way home, all I could think of was a scene where a spider the size of Texas chased two characters around, all that semen-thick silk, death venom, a child rapist's fangs. Mom was sobbing, and dad leaned one foot over to take hold of me and bring me onto their island. Now we could be scared of the ground together. My father kissed my forehead while my mother ran her fingers through my hair, her wedding ring cutting my scalp. No words were said. Words of love and hope nev-

-er existed between us, but maybe in this instance, although unlikely, they were feeling more than just fear for the spiders, but also guilt for never being there and relief that I was safe with them now, in their painful grip. But I wanted to let go. I was just as scared as my parents, yet I wanted to let go. Let go. Safe. Safe. A faggot child can never be safe in this world. A boy that's been raped has had his string cut in half. A drop in the ocean that left no ripple. An arctic calm. When I opened my eyes, I was on my side on top of the kitchen island, and my mother was still holding me as if to pull me back into her womb, a lost wish to start over again, with no trauma, pure innocence. Dad put a plastic popcorn bucket over both spiders and a pack of batteries on top to weigh it down. When I climbed off the island and placed my ear to the plastic I could hear them struggling to escape through the tiles. That's what Riley must have felt like before he first touched me, that internal reaching, and that's what he must have felt, the stake through the heart, knowing he could never feel the inside of my body ever again if he had been caught alive.

X   X   X

We stood in single-filed lines with one shoulder against the wall, eyes to the back of another student's head, and marched quietly as if we were prisoners being taken to our cells, like pigs being processed for execution. All it would take is a whisper or one student breaking formation, and then a teacher would bark orders at us, threatening time-outs, detentions, being separated and alone during lunch, or worse, being banned from recess. A girl once told me that I'd grow up to shoot up a school, even though I was afraid of guns. Yet, I felt that if a shooter came through the door, my body would be the first to be ripped to shreds by a magazine of bullets. This is the Wild West. There were the cowboy boots that I only wore on Friday, sprayed with blood, the worthless school shooting nursery rhymes taped to a cabinet that was filled with colored papers and markers and crayons and glue, a piece of my skull that could have jammed into it, something the world could see like pornography, a limp dick, desensitized to yet another Texas massacre. I yanked my shoulder back from the wall, took three steps to my left, and didn't care what the teachers did to me. They were never there to teach me. Once they realized I was left-handed, it didn't matter if I could read at a higher level; my handwriting was shit, and I should be punished and left out of specific lessons. At one point, they placed me in special education for an entire month because I refused to make my handwriting neater. That meant I must have been a fucking idiot. What would they have cared if I were shot to death? What if they had known that I was gone for three weeks the previous year because I tried to kill myself? Get back in line, faggot. Hide under that desk. Get in the closet. Stay silent. No matter what, dead as fuck.

X   X   X

The teachers had all the fifth-grade boys stuffed into a single classroom, and they played a VHS tape that told us what would happen to our bodies. Other kids laughed and blushed. Girls develop quicker than boys. Don't be scared if you wake up and the sheets are sticky. Here's an adult penis. This is how a baby is made. No body is the same. There was no conversation about what it might be like for two men together; gay people didn't exist except within jokes. Either way, the video left me horny and angry, wanting more to understand what I might be, less what I had to pretend to be or what I had to hide.

After the presentation, fire alarms went off, and the teachers told us to hide in closets and under desks. One kid was ordered to turn off the lights, and then we were told to stay silent. Not so funny anymore. There weren't any doors to our elementary classrooms, so it wasn't authentic when the mock-shooter dressed in full body armor with an assault rifle entered our classroom only to leave a few seconds later as if we weren't notably hiding and soaked in our piss. In reality, we'd all be dead, and one of us would have grown up to be the shooter, knowing every worthless part of the drill. As I hid in a closet, fitting for a bullied faggot, it occurred to me that I might someday die with my brains scattered all over the desk behind me, way before I ever grow any pubes or experience my first real cum.

After our school shooting death simulation drill, we pledged allegiance to the American and Texas flags and then headed to science class with the thoughts of being mass murdered and our cocks getting bigger at the forefront of our minds. There were tall mesh nets on top of our desks with butterflies fluttering around inside them. We learned about the cycle of life in humans and metamorphosis in insects. I must have done something wrong because my butterfly kept flapping against the net as if to escape or harm itself. Stupid like the bird that banged against my bedroom window the previous night before it died from internal

bleeding. I didn't feel any different than these creatures; I was already going through my own metamorphosis from a bruised ceramic boy with a halo to a
feral wolf with pleasure fangs built for grinding canine teeth and corruptive sex. Their butterflies knew
when to rest and boast the patterns on their wings, but
that beauty isn't enough to prevent them from being
snuffed out of their short-lived existences. Yes, I knew
mine would die first, and people would make fun of
me for it, the possibility of my queerness somehow
causing its death. Some of the girls would also cry
once their winged pet died. One would even bury it in
the dirt near the playground during recess. But I'd give
more affection toward mine in its life and death than
any of them ever could. None of the other kids could
understand that feeling of being trapped in the neon
green net, living for other's pleasure with no escape,
and then you're dead, flushed away, forgotten.

It rained heavily in all directions for half of recess.
For the first half, I sat inside with my friend, Jasmine,
one of the few black kids at school, meaning the
school of mostly white and Latino kids ignored her.
I'd read a handful of pages out of a book, hand it
over to her, and then she'd read out loud to me. When
we got bored, when the storm clouds had begun to
paint bronze over heaven, we snuck into the miniature
greenhouse. She would rest on the ground, like always,
sometimes staring at the plants, while I felt around
in the soil to let the worms swarm over my hands. I
didn't understand why people found slimy creatures
ugly, whereas I meditated on their innocence. One
day, I would be in a tiny wooden coffin, and bugs
would clean the hurt inflicted on me, leaving only my
feeble candy butterscotch bones. Skulls don't frown.
Bones are forever preserved with care and respect as

if they were art, while the flesh is hated by its owner and the rest of the world until it has formed into its final state of ugly rot.

When the rain forced the rest of the kids back into the school, everyone took up every last computer, leaving a few of us to venture to the library. That was fine by us. Jasmine and I could stumble for books between bookcases in dim light to the sound of water dancing on the glass rooftop. The universe was beginning to swallow me inside the library and on posters thumb-tacked to the wall in our science class. I stared at pictures I printed of star clusters, nebulas, moons on other planets, and anywhere else I desperately wanted to venture. By venture, I meant that I wanted to melt and disintegrate and become a star, my ice or rock molecules making up a piece of Saturn's rings or an explosion that'd form a black hole. My metamorphosis continued to take new alien forms that I knew were separating me further from the other kids. No longer just a faggot, I'd become a freak, too.

A week later, I remember Jasmine asking if I could get a book off her desk during recess, so I went back inside the school and quietly made my way into the classroom. I noticed my English teacher bent down, doing something with poster paper, unaware I was behind her. People at school always found it funny that anytime someone tried to scare me, I'd scream, jump, and then rattle as if the fear were trying to throttle me out of my body. So I went up behind her, inhaled deeply, and scared her. "Ah!" That's all I had screamed. A split second of my raised voice jolted her up, and then she screamed, too, causing me to cry just as loudly. My body started shaking, my heart racing, and I could feel sets of hairy adult hands on my skin, from my chest to my waist.

"What the fuck is wrong with you, D?" She stuttered her words, held out scissors in front of me, and moved closer as I crawled backward on the carpet. "You could have fucking killed me. Do you realize I was cutting paper with scissors? I could have slashed my throat open! Is that funny to you?"

"No, no, it's not funny. I'm sorry. I thought you'd like that. Some people, they like to be scared."

"What's so funny about being scared? Am I laughing? Are you laughing? You're in school. Nothing is funny. You're here to learn. Why can't you be like the other kids and play outside with them? You almost fucking killed me! Get up. Stand up! Your parents are going to find out about this. Think about that. Think about what they'll do to you when you get home."

With one shoulder brushing against the wall, I followed behind her to a closet-sized room. She forcefully tossed me into it, my left shoulder banged against a printer, and then she ordered me to stay inside until she felt like I had learned my lesson.

I didn't need to turn the knob to know it was unlocked, but I remained inside because a part of me wanted to take the shame while the other part knew this was wrong. Gay kids find comfort hiding in closets. Now I was forced into one. There was a crevice between the wall and the tall, bulky printer. I slid my emaciated body through it until I naturally curled up into a ball where I thought nobody would be able to find me, where I could no longer exist, and maybe my teacher would forget about me, they'd lock down the school, and I'd die in a nest of cobwebs and dust. Boy as a tarantula trapped under the popcorn bucket. But one of the other teachers came in and managed to find me. Her head was still towering over me as I retraced my head from out of my shirt, drenched in snot and tears. Nobody should walk in on a faggot when it's sulking in its own closet.

"You should be ashamed of yourself," she scolded, even though she knew I was sorry. "I know how you're going to grow up. Just like any other boy. Violent. Lonely. Abusive. Nobody is ever going to pity you. So stop crying. I can't imagine what your parents go through. Dealing with such a terrible kid."

A door slammed a thousand times that day. An echoing noise from the past and reverberation into death. I left the room, but every other space transformed into a different kind of closet.

Where is everyone? Iridescent butterflies were kissing my hands. I had released them all from their playful science class traps and led them to the greenhouse by the playground. All the other kids were showing off books they got from the Scholastic book fair; I had none because I was poor without realizing it or even comprehending the concept of poverty. *They think they're so cool because they can play hot cross buns on a recorder.* I kicked a water fountain wrapped in a clear plastic bag until it wstarted leaking at the bottom of the sac while the other kids sang in the music room after watching a film about Beethoven. All their stupid expensive Eye Spy and Junie B. Jones books under their feet.

X   X   X

It's not your fault that you didn't see the warning signs; it happened to you, and you wanted him to be safe so badly that you wouldn't allow yourself to believe it could be true. If I take the power and monitor cords away, he's going to unplug the ones attached to my computer while we're asleep and continue to play games all night. Cries over everything. Can't do anything. Can't get him to understand math problems. It's because he has your brain, not mine. He's emotional like you. Do you think I want to quit? I'm sick of this retail shit. Do you know how hard it is to fake a smile for sixty hours a week when all you can think about is your silent son becoming a maniac, knowing you can't help him or spend time with him because you have to work yourself to death? I'm getting fatter and fatter, and it's not just the fucking pregnancy, either. It will only worsen for all of us as he gets older and realizes what happened to him. You can't punish him. I need a vacation from him again. Can't you send him back to your mother's for a month? Are we bad parents? If I ground him from the TV, he will spend it reading books from school, and we can't take that from him. I can't raise my voice, or else we could get in trouble. If I raise my voice, he jumps back like you do, and I hate that look both of you give me. The other kids call him a faggot at school, so is it that big of a surprise if he says the word fuck out of anger while crying at daycare? You're the one always screaming fuck during the football games. He doesn't need therapy. It'll only traumatize him more. So you think he should remain like this?

X   X   X

We sheltered inside the indoor playroom at the day-care, all of us elementary kids, and clamored around in the darkness to watch the Disney animated version of Robin Hood. J sat beside me, as always, and found himself trapped underwater with cybernetic aliens in his *Metroid Fusion* Game Boy game. "Help me with this," he'd bug me and tap my kneecap. But I couldn't take my mind off the fox on the box TV being tied up and faced with the erotic possibility of death. As I watched the film, I rubbed myself and felt the storm outside vibrate its electricity through my blood. On the right side, Luke was drawing in his sketchbook. He was my newest friend, a naturally talented artist and nerdy ginger with a Padawan hair braid inspired by the Star Wars sequels that his parents let him grow out. Everything Luke drew was violent and inspired by horror films. That day, he sketched the Chucky doll being stabbed by Michael Myers from the Halloween movies.

Most of the other kids panicked when the teach-ers went out and the tornado sirens began to sing. The torrential wind shook the building as children cramped together in whispered worries. I gazed around the room and dissociated while staring at the kids, animals, and balloons painted on the walls. Ta-rantulas were exiting through spores and rupturing through the vents. The world became virtual. Silver. A dim light in a vacant classroom. Ghost children lost in tiny, smelly bathrooms. The tornadoes would never arrive to gyrate our bodies into eviscerated flesh flat-tened by rubble and trash, but the fear that this place would soon be leveled into unrecognizable shit would persist.

Dad needed to focus on caring for my newborn sister, and my mother had to work overnight because the Victoria's Secret was being remodeled for the next season's wear. After a few calls, it was decided I'd go to Luke's home for a sleepover. The storm died down after it hailed for half an hour, but the clouds were still spiraling through an emerald sky, M43 Orion Falls space canvas melting. We fought in the backyard with plastic lightsabers, feet in the tall wet grass, the post-rain scent filling our lungs, and construction outside the Raytheon facility nearby was finally halted thanks to the fear of constant tornadoes. When we battled, I always allowed myself to lose and die; I liked to play the part of the Sith because I saw myself as corrupted, and for someone like me, death would be my only form of redemption.

He showed me a Star Wars comic his parents bought him, where all the protagonists were kids. In this one, a boy turns to the dark side after realizing that he's a fag or whatever and kills one of his best friends that became a Jedi. Near the end, a little girl blows up one of his hands, but he survives, still holding onto his red lightsaber with the other hand as he walks alone through a mountainous landscape. I'd steal the comic from him and masturbate furiously to it the next day. I'd fantasize that I was the boy that fell from grace, a black leather suit squeezing my skin, murdering my friends, my masturbation hand exploding, he becomes a Sith because he's gay like me, he suffers because to be gay is to hurt.

We were in his bedroom, hiding behind his bed that faced the wall, kneeling as we went through his sketchbooks and magazine collages scattered on the carpet. His parents must have been sex freaks because he was able to steal dozens of pornographic magazines out of their room without them knowing. Skinny white girls fucking themselves with their fingers, getting fucked from both sides with a cock in their mouths, semen drizzling from hair and face, sex-crazed eyes like a psychotic gaze, women whipped, caned, cunt fisted, candlewax on tits, black latex suits, submissive and dominant, bound by rope, tits and cocks pierced, piss, and vomit. My left index finger covered the face of the tied-up girl, and I uttered to him without thinking, "I want to be tied up like that." My mind and cock were too busy reimagining the Robin Hood movie scene, wanting to be that fox, fox as a boy, the boy tied up, soon to be raped and punched and knocked against a coffee table, his vision and nose permanently altered.

"You mean you want to tie her up?" Luke went with what he imagined I must have meant to say and then talked about the girls. "I want to fuck her so bad. Which one do you like best? Not that girl. She's ugly."

When you realize you're gay, the first lie you tell is how a flurry of snowflakes eventually transforms into a destructive blizzard. You say which girls you like and how you want to suck her breasts, but you can't detail how you find them attractive. As you lie to your friend's face, you will also imagine wanting to have sex with him while hating them for being normal. But sometimes, you slip, they see into you, and you realize you've ruined things for good.

"Honestly, they're all kind of ugly. Can't you show me more of your drawings?"

We fell asleep in his bed to a *Nightmare on Elm Street* sequel movie. Between us were our lightsabers. He wore a single Freddy Krueger glove on one hand that he got from Party City for Halloween last year. Suddenly, the VHS tape went to static, trillions of tiny flashing dots blinking to the sound of white noise, and even though it scared me, I didn't want to turn off the TV. I stared at him and saw the dots dance on his face as he rested, like rain coming down at relentless speed on a dead body. I fell asleep and into another wormhole, Cygnus X-1 dog mouth open wide with squid ink.

Goosebumps was on when I woke up. Luke sat up on the bed and moved his arms around as a pet tarantula crawled over his freckled skin. At first, I was entranced by it, but I fell off the bed and felt my body freeze as it moved closer. It wasn't me that I felt in my body; I felt the terror raging inside my mother. Scared of everything. Everything a monster.

"It's okay, D. It won't hurt you. I'll, uh, I'll put her away. Sorry. I didn't realize…." When Luke returned, he asked me without looking into my eyes, "D, are you gay or something? It's okay if you are… I won't tell anyone. My mom likes both, so… I won't hate you like others would."

What had given it away? My disinterest in his collages that he stole from his horny parents or my fear of the spider? Either way, I nodded my head, and then he smiled back at me.

The next day that we met at daycare, I gave him an origami box while we were in the art room. My dead butterfly was inside of it. As I had hoped, he was bewildered and excited to see the bug's corpse. He rubbed the wings gently, and they accidentally came off. I explained, "It's a gift for you being such a good friend to me. I thought you could tape it to the last page of your sketchbook, so one day when we're older, and we're not able to hang out as much, or one of us moves away, you'll see it, and you'll remember me."

Before we exited the game room, he made sure to tape it to the last page and placed the detached wings back where they should have been.

A week later, Luke moved away, and I never saw him again. I thought being gay might be normal after the sleepover with him, but then he was gone, and a day later, I drank sour milk at daycare and vomited everywhere, and everyone was calling me a stupid loser weirdo faggot gaywad all over again. Burrowed into the tarantula's nest, tied up, and taped together to preserve my fragile limbs.

TEXAS

CHAINSAW

Like my parents, I failed my child. I said I'd do everything not to become them, and then I became them.
*Give him the stability you didn't have, feed him, and keep him
safe.* We go without dinner for another night. Even
when we remain in the same house, the city zoning
laws move him to a different school every year. *If
only you knew what I went through. If only you knew
how good you have it. What do you have to cry about?* These
damaging words my father said to me that I spat on
my child.

In time, he will learn to retaliate and hate me, as he
should, but I will continue to fight for his respect. I
will repeatedly say the wrong things and fuck up, and
because of this, he will kill himself. If he's already attempted it once, it's only a matter of time before he
does it again more efficiently. I know this because my
parents had driven me to suicide before I gave birth
to him.

One day, I will walk into my son's bedroom. He will
have started puberty, and the trauma will have manifested into every part of his being. The triggers and
nightmares will attack him every hour of the day. His
mind will only think of fight or flight. He will stop
feeling comfortable in his body and begin cutting,
burning, and punching it. Eventually, he will turn to
drugs. The lethal combination of self-harming while
under the influence of pain medication will lead him
to pass out on the carpet, having fallen out of his
computer chair, and I will find him there, green ash
tree angel rotting, in his ocean of blood, I nail the
coffin shut.

His father won't understand until after he's dead, as
he doesn't now. *He doesn't need therapy. Boys like to be left*

alone. Did you like being around your parents? Maybe he's not reacting like you expect him to because he's not traumatized. He is fragile glass shattering in slow motion, and there's nothing we can do to prevent his inevitable death.

X   X   X

I wake up from a nightmare, reimagining my suicide attempt from when I was sixteen. I remember leaning over the edge of the school's rooftop and feeling so frustrated that I wasn't scared of the ground. It was as if life was telling me that this was the only comprehensible answer left. Others would have gone back downstairs. They would have cut themselves with a dull knife. I jumped. What I must have been thinking at that moment, meditating on the slight breeze that shook the shrubs, or the impressionist painting of the Midwest cornfields, the taste of soybeans still in my mouth. It could have been any of those memories, like those plaguing me as I squeeze the plastic telephone at the kitchen table. I can't believe I let this happen. How did I not see a single fucking sign? If I could have killed the fucking piece of shit pedophile myself, squeeze his neck with this cord that's tied around my fingers, and fucking smash his sick fucking brains out. I don't want to blame myself for it now; I practically blame myself for what happened with each passing breath leading me to the grave. So it's mom that I must spite and humiliate.

When she picks up, I'm a zombie grunting like a drunk, but I promise I'm sober when I scathe her, "Do you remember when I was six years old, and we were living in North Dakota? I used to…

take the bus home from elementary school. I'd sit there in the trailer, eating peanut butter sandwiches and a bag of chipsbeyond the sunset. That year, I lived in four states and went to three schools. Have you ever thought... How terrible the two of you were? Do you remember when you made me fucking home-less while I was pregnant? You said that I was a slut, that I wouldn't amount to anything, but here I am. You're still terrible parents. Not even good grandpar-ents. Forget me. When was the last time you thought about D, anyway?"

"S..." Mom coos. "I don't know what to say."

I can hear her crying over the phone. G-d. I should have known that this would only make me feel worse. As I hear her break into a regretful sob, I slam my face into the table, rest my head, and imagine the sound of train tracks running over me. I can still remember, D, the day my water broke. There was only one hos-pital in the county. Even though we sped as fast as we could while I was falling into labor, we were stopped for an hour by trains coming in all directions. G-d, hear me. Let this boy be my salvation. 11:30 AM. June 7, 1994. It wasn't meant to be an accident. All threads lead to the center of the same net. Please. Hate me for as long as you must. Just don't leave me like I tried to do. You're too young to become an angel, but that doesn't mean you can't be worthy of spreading a life of grace.

X   X   X

My parents have been pipe-liners for almost thirty years. Destroyers of the earth. They drill holes into indigenous lands, risking violent death each day, and come home to their motor home with barely enough money to afford fast food. Their lives are centered around work, making money, and losing money. From my birth until I left the Midwest six months after D was born, I traveled and lived with them in more than forty states. There was no sightseeing, no time for tourism, vacation, settling down, and making best friends; I lived as a wayfarer and a mistake they had to drag along to whatever shit hole they went next Their payoff came when a job was completed, and we could go back home in our rusted and decaying rural Iowa town, and then they wouldn't have to work for two or three months.

Watch me leave without saying goodbye and someday prove I can be the parent I should've had when I grew up. I saw what both of you did wrong, so I know the best way to raise a child.

Five or six days out of the week, clocking in at fifty to sixty-five hours, I've been distilled by my parents' same toxic work mentality. Another day of seeing my son for thirty minutes, excluding the drive home from daycare and baseball practice. When I pick him up and see his disinterest in himself and me, I let the apathy kick in and give up.

Life is a horror movie, and despite all the violence I witness, I'm the sole survivor, even though I'd rather have been the first one dead.

Customers look down on me as inferior because this is all I can be since I wasn't raised to be dressed in suits. How can I prove to them that I am human as I fold more stacks of lingerie that they toss to the floor? Watch me remain pure of heart and dig my way out of this to become something far wiser, wealthier, and sexier than any of them.

Sometimes, when the mall is slow and nobody's shopping, I end up staring at the open door of my corporate store that gazes into another monotonous department, and I philosophize if any of the tiresome standing around has any meaning. I think of some shit like, we could all be unique individuals that coexist and appreciate each other's beautifully complex identities. Instead, we're lost in the consumerist shopping mall buried in our unconscious mind that charades us with billboards, clothes, and plastic garbage. We think the shopping mall in our heads is the transcendent substitute for finding true meaning in life.

In the middle of work, while stocking bras at Victoria's Secret, a man jumps off the highest balcony of the mall. Everyone rushes out to see his corpse spattered across the ice-skating rink. And all I can think about is D. He typically goes to that skating rink when I can't afford to take him to daycare and have to bring him to work. I won't tell him about it, but he will somehow figure it out from someone at school or my job. When he finds out, it will plant an idea in his head, and I'll be stacking bras in a crowded store like I'm doing now. Then I'll hear the slam outside the store and see my angel boy shattered like glass on the frozen floor, pieces of him scattered everywhere in an unrecognizable mess.

The store didn't close that day. A half-hour later, the body had been shoved into a bag and taken away, the gore had been swept and soaked up, shoppers had either left or gone back to shopping, and I returned to work, shaking, thinking about when I jumped off a roof as a teenager and failed to die.

D was molested in a mall, and yet I kept working there. Oh, I'll just transfer to a different one. It's safer there. He doesn't care. It's not like he even remembers it. Something like that would never happen again to him. It's so rare, anyway, especially to boys, isn't it? Then again, when I was a kid, everyone was raped and abused or had been a rapist and an abuser. But that was Iowa, that was nowhere, and this is the city; we came here to escape all that. And yet the corruption is inescapable.

Another award from the company means more money. Money is worth dying for if it means giving your child food so he can continue going to the daycare he hates. Yes, my life is expendable for clothes made in sweatshops and prisons. When people would rob our store and hold knives or guns at my employees and me, I'd chase after them until the mall officers caught up to arrest them. Some days when I'm at work, I imagine getting shot in the stomach and bleeding out slowly or getting shot in the face, and the brutal manner of my murder is how I'd be remembered. I'm at work, folding panties and sorting dresses, and thinking about my helpless son getting shot to death in school, while I could be shot to death in the mall, and how he was raped by someone I trusted while I was busy working and not thinking or noticing, and how I was busy shopping while he was being molested in the hidden guts of a mall.

X　　　　　　　X　　　　　　　X

A few hours after I get off a late shift, one of the teachers at D's school calls to inform me that he's gotten sick on the first night of the science camp trip. They're out in the middle of rural nowhere two hours away and tell me that I need to pick him up tonight because they can't let him sleep in his room while he's sick, and they have too much to do in the morning. D's father guilt trips me into picking him up since he has to work earlier, and now he makes more money than me. So I print off the directions to the camp, read them over in the car, and cruise on the vacant highway.

Folded-up papers in one hand and the steering wheel in the other. The roads become more desolate with fewer streetlights. Each turn bends over itself and into a new void. It only grows darker with each passing minute. When D gets sick, he hallucinates, hurts himself, and sobs madly. He needs me, but I feel like I'm only driving further away from him. I put the car in park and attempt to go through the printed-out steps and recall where I've gone, but it's too late at night to think properly.

When I look back up, I notice a man wearing a horrifying plastic mask resembling a skinned face and holding a revved-up chainsaw. I scream and remember the movie that he's dressed up from and slam on the wheel, and then he's chasing after me. Like in a horror movie, I spend way too much time hyperventilating and looking up at the rear-view mirror and almost slam the car into a tree. But when I slow down, he's closer to the back of the truck, and then I'm screaming again. I get away. I'm driving as fast as I can down dirt roads with no signs or lights in my way. The gas tank is getting low. Living a nightmare. This is how

I'm going to die. Manager at a Victoria's Secret is slain, skinned, and cannibalized in a small rural white-trash Texas town. Son dies in his teacher's arms, vomiting to death.

When I think I've found my way again, I suddenly hear the chainsaw crackling and grinding too close to the car. Still, I can't see him anymore, and then I'm driving in circles, throwing the papers with directions around, crying to G-d, cursing at my parents, and attempting to tear the wheel out of the car as my back bends into my seat. He's gone, and I'm finally seeing what was on the paper, but the gas is too low, and I don't even want to go home. I want to take D with me to a hotel and sleep there for the night. I want to squeeze him until he does the same to me and pretend we're not in Texas anymore while I click my shoes together. I'll take you wherever you want, D. Saturn, here we come.

By the time I pick D up, he's running a fever, vomited everything out of his stomach, and has scratched his arms bloody. I sit with him in the car outside the camp, listen to his grueling sobs, and all I can do is stare at the lake and think about driving us into it. The kids forced him to drink spoiled milk, and another kid put mayo and mustard on his burger. D's not used to all that greasy shit. Then they made fun of him for getting sick. "Please put me in a different school," he begs. "I want to start over. They used to like me… Why does everyone hate me? Why can't I stop being a fucking retard?" If I weren't paralyzed by the fear of being bisected on the way home, I would have slapped him and told him not to use those words, and then he'd just cry and hate me even more.

He shivers and aches more as I begin driving home. "How much longer? Mom, please." I look at the clock—almost two in the morning now. "I need to go to the bathroom. I'm gonna, please. I don't want to go in the car." Once I find a gas station, I finally feel like I can exhale. I kiss him on the forehead and walk with him to a dumpster so he can pee. Afterward, he sits back in the passenger seat and vomits into a plastic bag as I look for my wallet. I leave the radio on with the windows down as I get gas. There's no wind, only the cool settled air of a hole in nowhere, transmuting the same Stone Temple Pilots grunge song playing for the hundredth time this week.

The second I turn around after putting the nozzle into the tank, I hear the click of the safety being taken off a gun, and then it's the lips of the gun pressed to my forehead. He speaks before me and asks for my flip phone and wallet, but before I can say anything, he notices me shift and steps away before yelling at me, commanding that I don't move. "I threw my wallet in my seat," I explain and begin to beg. "Please, I'm pregnant, and my son is sick and in the car. I'll give you what you want, but please don't hurt us. Look, I get it. We're poor, too."

"Don't fucking move! I'll get it. I'll shoot your fucking kid if you do, and then I'll shoot you."

But my motherly instincts betray me as I turn around to see if D is okay, and then he fires his gun through the car's open windows. D doesn't make a sound, so I can only figure he's dead. Once he grabs my wallet, he asks for my phone, so I hand it to him with my eyes swollen and blinded with tears, and then he fires again, maybe up in the air, and I feel my heartbeat jump out of my chest as my body throttles itself back against the car. I open my eyes, and he's gone. D still hasn't made a sound.

"Oh my G-d. Oh my G-d. I can't do this. Please, G-d. Don't take him."

I gaze into the open window. D's holding onto his left ear, and his upper body is spinning in circles with a droning look in his eyes. Suddenly, his pupils expand, and he collapses into his seat, chest between legs, head hanging down, and hair almost touching the plastic vomit bag. When I reach for where I expect to find my flip phone, I forget it was stolen. At least the tank is full now.

X   X   X

One day, my son will ask me, "Why Texas?" Why this terrible red state with no Jews, and now you know I'm gay and a rape victim, and you expect me to thrive in this environment when you were never around to give me the emotional support I needed? And I won't know what to say because I asked my parents the same question about Iowa when my grandparents could've settled in a place like New York or at least Chicago or whatever. I know it's not the best place, but it was the first one to give us a chance; even if we had to eat the worms in the dirt to have an opportunity that wasn't WIC and food stamps, we could make this ours, somehow, the Lone Star can be our Magen David. Just kidding, that's a bad joke, and he will still say,

"Why Texas," and then, "I fucking hate both of you."

I'm giving him a sister nine years later after he was born. If he's still alive in the coming years or a decade (past twenty seems unimaginable), she will grow up with vague images of him in a mental hospital, sobbing, carvings on his arms and legs, the long drives back and forth to group therapy, the drugs, the skunky pot smoke on his clothes, slamming the door at three in the morning, his mother realizing that to raise a daughter, she must sacrifice giving her firstborn any form of help, because he will be too far fucked to ever recover from everything that has happened and will continue to happen to him. And even though he wanted a sister, he would hate her, baring jealousy that he knows is selfish to have, and it will make him hate his father and me more.

X   X   X

In utero, through your night terrors, the self-harming, collapsing in the kitchen to crawl into a sphere, I will hold you through it all. Cry into my shoulder until I've become your River. Until I've become your Kyle. Your Jon. I'll carry your weight when your shoulders ache and you've gone days without sleeping. I knew you before you were born and have followed your path further than where you are now. Survive, keep hope, and know that I love you. I'd have myself chainsawed to pieces and take every bullet in the world for you.

My son, who won't allow himself to be touched by anyone. Even love horrifies him. He doesn't understand why his body reacts the way that it does. When I hold him, he must see me as a literal mold of steaming coiled excrement. Eventually, the touch he felt with

Riley and the stranger inside the mall will be the only thing that feels real to him. He will become addicted to it until it destroys him.

After he finds me sobbing on the top of the toilet seat in the guest bathroom, his father sees him hiding under the computer table with a kitchen knife, ready to stab him in case he raises his voice at me again. Then I'm told I need to punish him for this, so I dismantle his Lego sets piece by piece, throw them in the trash, and say that I got rid of them because he needs to grow up and stop being a kid. You can't just stab your daddy to death because he was rightfully fighting your mom.

"Get this through your fucking head. I fucking hate you." D cries his words with disappointment instead of anger. "You're the worst mother ever."

X   X   X

The mall's empty of customers. Not even muzak is playing yet, and the morning shift workers barely make a sound as they prepare to open their stores. I find a random table in the food court and take in the smell of everything I can't afford. Across from me is the Barnes & Noble, where D prefers to spend his time; he reads and asks me to buy him books, but I can't, so I just let him read there. On the opposite side of the bookstore is Dave and Buster's game store, where he's saving up tickets to win a lava lamp. I sit alone and call my mother, and I tell her what D said to me when I threw away his Legos and that I'm sorry for hating her and Dad so much and that I want to forgive and maybe things can get better. I'm no longer thinking about what happened at the ice-skating rink. Instead, I imagine the day that D survives all of the trauma that will scathe him and that he will apologize for having hated me for so long.

DEATH

SCENE

You don't forget your first funeral. For me, it was my great-grandfather on my dad's side. I only met him three or so times, but I still cried, and I don't know why I did. Mom was surprised that I understood the concept of death so quickly. *If you tell her, I swear I'll fucking kill you. You love me, right?* Kids comprehend more than adults can ever realize. Some kids experience more trauma than most people might witness throughout their entire lives. "Since Dad's side is Christian, does that mean great-grandpa is a pile of ashes now? Did they burn his corpse? I don't get why they do that, mom. It seems really mean. You're not going to burn my corpse when I die, will you?" Mom told me I wouldn't be dying for a while, and no, she wouldn't burn my corpse. From what I knew, my body would be gently placed into a cheap wooden coffin, nailed shut, and then transform into a cosmic mikveh churning with rotting guts that bugs would devour.

My memories of great-grandpa: the good one, the bad one, and then his death. He and my great-grandma lived in an old farmhouse with crops that went on for miles. I remember a night of fireworks, fireflies in mason jars, the out-of-tune piano in the basement, all these family members I never knew who lived eight hundred miles from me and that I'd never see them ever again, one of my uncles getting trashed and forced to leave after getting in a fistfight. And I remember grandma taking me with her to see him and an argument she had with him that had her wailing and screaming on the way back to her house. Great-grandpa told her, "You don't mean shit to me. You have a faggot for a son, drug addict kids, a boy who knocked up a girl and ran away from you, and you're fucking divorced. Your entire life is a fucking failure. Get the fuck out of my house. I don't want to see your face

ever again." Then there was a box containing his ashes, and grandma wailed as they were lowered into a
hole in the ground.

Why do you cry for those who have hurt you when
they die? Behind those tears, do you still hate them, or
is it more complicated than that?

X   X   X

On the way home from the funeral in Iowa, I remembered what dad said to grandma about G-d and angels
not being real, and so I asked him while he was driving, "Is great-grandpa in heaven now?"

"What do you think, D? What you believe matters
more than anyone else, as long as you don't push
those beliefs onto others."

I squeezed my I-Spy book and gazed out at the razed
homes of Kansas, recently hit by a tornado, and responded, "But if what someone believes isn't true,
then that means they're either lying or a dummy. I
think he's in heaven… But, maybe he's in hell, because… One time he was really really mean to grandma."

What I really meant to say was, 'Maybe heaven is
empty, the earth is flooded with ghosts, and hell is
the boiling soup that most of us are sent to for being
dummies and liars.'

Dad turned down the radio, even though one of
mom's favorite songs was playing. She listened to The

Cult's 'Painted on My Heart' practically every day until not even the toothpaste trick could clean all the scratches on the Gone In 60 Seconds soundtrack CD. I asked, "Mom, do you want me to play this song at your funeral after you're dead?"

She chuckled, put on her sunglasses, and wiped away tears before quickly answering, "No, not this one. I think, maybe something by Metallica." Then she nodded as if she knew the song, yet she couldn't tell me. "But I don't want a funeral. Some friends and family at the house, and burn me."

While she was talking, dad was speaking over her, saying I was right about something and beginning to take on his beliefs. Once she was done, he went on a clear, deadpan tone, "Heaven is a logical concept to create since humans are scared of death; it's in our nature to want to survive for as long as we can. But the truth is… None of it is real. You close your eyes and see static and black, but death is even less than that. Death isn't even emptiness. It's beyond what any of us can comprehend. Great-grandpa, he might have lived his life in devotion to G-d, praying that when he'd get to heaven, it'd be this eternal cloud where everyone is already there. But the truth is that he's dead, like the animals we eat, like roadkill, like an ant being stepped on. Humans are no more special than any other creature. He's gone, and it'll eventually be as if he has left no trace and never existed on this planet. I'll start losing memories of him. Eventually, everyone that once knew him will be dead, too. That's the true instance of death. People think there's an endless heaven; I think there's an endless nothingness."

A few hours later, mom was messing with the radio

and a song came on. At first, she was going to change it, but dad insisted that she keep it on. I'd heard him listen to it before on the computer through Windows Media Player as the program's sound visualizer generated ethereal colors and nebulous shapes to the music. It was Aerosmith's, 'Dream On'. Dad told me that a friend of his died in a car crash when he was a teenager and the song played at the funeral, so when it came on the radio, it always made him think about him. But I didn't know what that meant, nor did I mean to ask. Did it make him think about their friendship or solely his death? I couldn't imagine my friends like J or Jasmine dying in a car crash, but I could see myself in it quite clearly. Each car that passed by, I started to imagine that it was meant to slam right into me.

The song made me wonder if dad was really talking about his friend earlier and not great-grandpa. Was dad already beginning to lose memories of him? Had he already accepted that he'd never see him again, or did faint memories of them playing baseball still haunt him? What was left of his friend? Who was left to remember him?

As I was lost in thought about this person and slowly being haunted by the opening guitar chords of the song looping in my head, dad told me, "Even though he's gone, and I don't believe in heaven, your mom and I found a way to make sure that he lives on longer. We named you after him. You'll keep the memory of him for us and many others for a while, D."

"So I'm... I'm a car crash. Or a ghost. Aren't I?"

Dad put pressure on the brakes, pulled the car over, and then my memory goes blank, like hundreds of pounds of soil that would someday be piled over my coffin.

X   X   X

We had made it back home and I stared at the glow-in-the-dark stars glued to my ceiling as I contemplated what dad told me about what happens when we die. In between my stars was black paint on the plaster, which would be the universe. I imagined a void within my ceiling representing one hundred and sixty five light years of space, and that would be my body after death. And then I considered heaven as a possible hyperspace, quantum realms, how breath and consciousness could be what stabilizes the ether, the vibrant light from outside my window riding its separate waves, and where its propagation medium and magnetic field were formed from, time as the basking fluid wafting in my lava lamp. Death, when ego and identity evaporate, and what becomes distant in the afterlife is suddenly insignificant.

It was so hot outside that the power would shudder; it was only a matter of time before the neighborhood hit a blackout. My lava lamp, like a campfire coming to a flicker and to ash. I couldn't comprehend what was real anymore. I was convinced I had already lived and died several times, that I could have been dad's best friend, who I was named after, or maybe anyone, like mom's cousin, or every living creature that has or would exist. But this time, in this body, I'd face my final death, and what dad believed would come true.

After D, it would be an endless, less than nothing.

X   X   X

Every summer, my parents would leave me at my grandma's house for a couple of weeks, the damned Christian side of my family, and then I'd spend those fleeting summer days with her or my uncles. It was my escape from Riley for a while until he was gone, and then, with the help of my uncles, it helped me shed my snakeskin.

While I was staying at grandma's, one of my three uncles briefly showed me a porn clip he downloaded on granny's computer of a skinny white girl sucking dick while getting fucked. It's normal to show pornography to a nine-year-old because a boy needs to know as early as possible that women are just mindless sex objects. After downloading the Cannibal Corpse and Deicide discography onto a CD, he closed out the video. I imitated the singer as best as possible, growling into a fist as if it were a microphone, and headbanged with my uncle N until I hallucinated stars. We sang improvised lyrics about killing and fucking women. Now I was earning his respect. More importantly, I was becoming more and more straight every day.

Uncle R was parked in the driveway for eons and smoking out of a glass pipe while nodding his head as a Metallica song blasted out of his speakers as loud as possible. Once he got out of the car and came into Grandma's house, he ran into the computer room, knowing I'd be there, reading about astronomy or playing flash games on the computer. Then he wres-

-led me, threw me around, smothered my face to the point that I could barely breathe, and lifted me into his burly chest for a hug before throwing me across the room and at the computer chair. My uncles wrestled me and laughed, and I guess it was fun, but they only acted like this because they were high on meth.

I got in the car's passenger seat and watched my uncles smoke a joint I thought was some skunk-smelling cigarette. Then we drove to the local pool with windows down, music blaring obnoxiously, and my eyes set on admiring them. They were artists, writers, musicians, and painters, and I wanted to be like them. The previous year, my uncle R's ex-girlfriend made me an oil painting of my favorite Pokemon, Entai. I hadn't realized it then, but they were drunk and stoned. Before we left the vehicle, one of my uncles offered me a swig of liquor, which I took fearfully, imagining that it would kill me.

Since Grandma was working, I went back to the house my three uncles and a friend were renting. They let me spray paint canvases with stencils in the garage and showed me their books of poetry. I watched Stargate SG-1 on the TV in the basement as they toked out of a bong and recorded sludgy drone metal songs onto cassettes. Uncle R let me see his bedroom while he edited music on his computer; the walls were covered in writing from markers and spray paint, a conglomeration of lyrics, paranoid thoughts, and general word salad. There were used syringes all over the table, but I figured it must have been due to some health issue.

Bored, I went upstairs and into my uncle R's bedroom, where he was watching Hellraiser: Deader. Chains bound a man with hooks, which pulled tight and rapidly, and then they tore apart his body, scattering his limbs all over the room, followed by chains ripping holes into other people. I stepped back from the TV, but my uncle placed a hand on my shoulder and told me to keep watching because his favorite part was coming up. A girl had begun to cry and stare at the carnage, then at Pinhead, before she plunged a machete right into her own stomach in slow motion. After she died, my uncle laughed hysterically, but I couldn't understand what was so funny. Suicide is... Ha ha, ha ha. He played the entire scene from beginning to end again, starting with the girl on a bed and the people that get killed egging her on to kill herself.

In the afternoon, I ate pizza in my swimming trunks and imagined going off the highboard a million more times. I lay on the sofa and nibbled on the hard crust while a ghost movie played on the TV. My innocent daydreaming had been replaced by fear of a ghost pulling my soul out of my chest. The film's protagonist kept listening to EVP recordings and trying to contact a vengeful spirit in his daughter's bedroom. In one scene, the protagonist is staring at TV static shaped like an enraged face. I'd seen that face before: In static and in others that looked down on me before... Riley was on the TV. I was in the movie, attempting to get back in contact with him. Static was his voice, his face, touch like electric shock, the scent of hot plastic melting, hardware vibrating.

My uncle's friend had come into the house and told them to hide everything. "The fucking cops are crawling around the house," he jittered as he spoke. "They're coming inside because they think we're hiding the guy who previously rented this place. Apparently, he broke out of prison."

"Fuck, what the fuck? Why would a guy who killed two girls go back to his old place and hide there? Why the fuck would we hide him?"

One of my uncles went outside to speak to the police officers, while the other two were rushing to hide anything that might get them arrested. A cop was eyeing me and asked uncle R who I was, then had me confirm that everything he said was true. I tried to hide on the sofa, but all I could imagine was us being shot and killed. When I looked at their guns, my mind recalled the robbery from when mom picked me up from the school camp, the gunshot permanently damaging and ringing in my ears. The shrill sound was blaring again, all to the tune of the ghost communicating with me on the TV.

After searching the house and finding nobody, and after my uncles cursing and digging up everything and smoking and drinking, we finished the movie. The spirit entered the man's body, which killed him, and then the film ended by zooming out on a photograph of him and his daughter smiling in front of a lake. I levitated in my sleep, into the film, and had woken up repeatedly, sweating in front of the crunching static on the monolithic screen, my body engulfed by its chaotic light, and I felt as if ghosts were surrounding me from every hallway, every corner of the room.

Dead girls were living down there, beneath the floor in the basement or maybe inside the drywall. A killer was on the loose. The windows were open, and for once, the warm breeze felt uninviting; the air took me out of myself and made me feel dispatched from the living world. With each passing day, I felt deader than before, and the hooks and chains were pulling at the meat in my flesh, yet I remained scared of the invisible and the shadows.

Mossy ectoplasm spilled out of my mouth while I slept. IC 417 Spider Web. Close-up shot. Glowing corpse stars swirl through rings of hazy fading memories. A boy angel, all drunk, drops from an asteroid and is pierced through his guts by Saturn's rings.

X   X   X

When I finally returned home, I began to sneak beers out of the fridge and fill liquor glasses to bring back to my bedroom. If I couldn't spend the night with J, I'd drink and watch cartoons or sometimes try to connect with my parents while staring into the droning violence on TV.

Most of the time, they watched X-Files, horror movies, or science fiction shows. I remember cuddling into my mother's lap while Mulder and Scully were chased around in a cold dark meat factory at night by a maniac with a butcher's knife. My mind drifted off into a dream where I found a copy of myself in the same slaughterhouse. Our school had just toured one a month ago. As I peeked out of a crevice between my fingers that covered my eyes, a cow's skull was crushed to dust by a machine. Now I was there, two worlds colliding, a boy as cattle for the slaughter, with frozen animal flesh stuck to hooks and chains from one side of a room to the other. Pinhead's voice echoed from a distance. I'd opened the box. Even though the lights were off, the machines were running, with severed arms, legs, and random slabs of animal flesh moving along the conveyer belt, ready to be sliced and cleaned into smaller pieces of death. After locking myself in a freezer room, I turned around to see a tall alien with pearly ebony eyes, the same kind I'd just seen in an X-File episode. It pierced a knife into my stomach and twisted it, and I felt it. When I woke up, I was still in my mother's lap, and Mulder and Scully were searching for other ghosts and extraterrestrial beings.

Whenever a bullet went off on TV, my heart would jump; I'd feel the memory, not just of what happened with the robbery, but with Riley, too. It wasn't affecting mom anymore. She'd heard gunshots and had people threaten to kill her throughout her entire life.

Drunk in bed, I tried to sleep through the sound of Jack Bauer on 24 firing off a hundred rounds from an assault rifle while he screamed at people before torturing them.

X   X   X

In one of my many fever dreams, I had done the most terrible thing. Jasmine and Sterling were sitting across from me at lunch, and even though there was no food in my lunchbox, it felt as heavy as my backpack. My pebble-sized fists were bludgeoning into my eyes as the tears flowed. They offered, "You can have some of our snacks, D." I told them, "I don't fucking care about rainbow sprinkled rice crispy treats or chocolate brownies wrapped in plastic. Nobody will ever understand." I took a gun out of the lunchbox and started shooting at the teachers. Once everyone began to panic, diving under tables, crawling to the doors, I jumped from seat to seat, scattering brains and breaking hearts, painting meal trays with gallons of blood. The carnage was endless and satisfying. I'd been told that this is what I'd be, despite being a harmless gun-fearing faggot. Who knew it felt better than attempting suicide? The police hadn't blown me away because I was a white kid, but that didn't prevent me from getting the death penalty. Once inside the death chamber, my legs, thighs, wrists, and chest were bound by leather straps. There was enough room on the trapdoor to fit three copies of nine-year-old me. Jack Bauer from 24 stood across from me with the hood in his hand and asked with distaste, "Any last words, you sick cunt?" I shook my head and stared through him with a determined scowl. The hood came over, then the noose, and with the snap of my neck, I had woken up from my mattress soaked in piss and sweat.

X   X   X

Something was beginning to take form—the violence of everything consumed almost all of my thoughts. I could recall deaths from every horror movie I'd seen, the screams characters made, and how satisfying it must have felt for the killer. My body had become volatile, a bomb, and nobody could touch it or come close to me without it detonating. Fear and stress pulsated with rapid energy through my blood.

It was during summer, I was ten years old, and none of my friends were at daycare that day. So I sat alone and suddenly realized what had been done to me, or at least what people thought had been done. And yet, it made no sense. *Why had I tried to kill myself again last summer? Because of him?* I loved him, but I hated my parents for not seeing what was happening or doing anything, but I hated him because he hurt me, but he loved me, and I hated myself because I wasn't supposed to like it or love him. What was all of it, then?

A staff member asked why I was sitting alone and not playing with the others. When I didn't answer, she reached for my shoulder. Without thinking, I frustratedly responded, "Don't touch me. Get away from me. I hate you. I hate this place."

"What did you say?" She raised her voice to prove her dominance as an adult over a child. "Don't talk like that ever again or else I'll tell your parents. If you continue this behavior, you'll be in time-out for the rest of the day."

"Go ahead and tell them. I hate them, too. I hate myself. I hate everything. I just want to die. I want to kill myself."

"You don't know what you're talking about. I'm not sure who you've been listening to that put those ideas in your head, but you're too young to have morbid thoughts like that."

My eyes focused on her throat. I thought about the teacher who said I almost killed her by scaring her, and then I thought about killing her. Like a vampire, I could bite down on her neck and suck on her geysers of gushing blood. When I'd die, I'd be dead like Riley, and people would hate me because I'm sick and evil, and then I'd be forgotten.

She put me in time-out for the rest of the day, which

meant I had to sit by her when we moved from class to class, including recess. It was also waterpark day. She had me change into my swimming trunks but told me I still had to sit on the bench with her while the others played. So I sat down and watched everyone get along, laughing and smiling as they danced while water sprinkled out of the ground. Kids shot water cannons at each other and pretended they were on two sides at war. Without J or my other friends there, I wouldn't have had anyone to play with, anyway. But I still smiled at the others having fun; they were so innocent, and I was so corrupted.

The staff member left long before my mother picked me up. I had gotten sick in the meantime and vomited outside the window on the way home. Mom squeezed the steering wheel as if she wanted to choke me to death and ground her teeth with force at the sight of seeing me sick. This meant she would have to take work off and fill in for shifts next week. When we got home, she asked, "Why do you always have to get sick, D? And why didn't you bring sunscreen? You knew what day it was."

As I tried to sip on the broth of some chicken noodle soup, mom tried to rub an aloe vera burn treatment over my body, but then I started to cry. The sticky liquid on my burning body made me think of Riley's hands. I started thinking about his dead body with the hole in his forehead. My body still burning like lit matches popping little fires over my skin. Or like great-grandpa getting cremated. "Stop touching me," I cried out. "You're hurting me!"

"Fuck, I'm sorry. I don't know how to do this any-more." Mom had begun to cry, panic, and pull on her hair while the sticky, smelly gel was stuck to her hands. "I'll never know how to help you."

A fever like a supernova radiated over my body while my skin stung from all touch from head to toes. The crying and the constant pain wouldn't stop. Outside of my room, bullets were being fired and people were screaming on the TV. The sound was festering like a nest of spiders and scorpions in my brain. I rolled around in my mess of sweat, snot, and spit and barely managed to vomit into a bucket in time before the bugs inside my head attacked again. There they were, crawling and festering in my bed, biting into my flesh, Riley's hands (*feels good, doesn't it? you like that?*), and then a bullet ripped through my head. I tried to minimize the pain by holding myself up from the tips of my fingers and toes, then fell onto my back to let the pain consume me, and when I looked to my bedroom door, a Cylon from Battlestar Galactica was marching into my bedroom. I screamed as loud as I could and in complete terror while the machine pointed a hand with guns attached to it at me. Dad was rattling my arms and trying to pull me out of the hallucination, but his body appeared half Cylon, and since his hands were on me, it only made me scream harder.

In my sleep, I felt something outside the dream tormenting my body. It dug into my skin, writhed under my sheets, and lathered along my peeling flesh. An obsidian black spirit sat close by and admired me as I slept. Blistering sun, blinding pale white, a skeleton warm from being fucked by the worst kind of evil. Solar flares of ejaculate. Face too hot to touch, but refreshing, hands of dark plasma surrounded the globe like distant satellites taking dirty pictures.

Once a harmless orb the size of a marble, the spirit
transformed itself into a body of venomous smoke. It
traced across familiar rooms that also felt distant and
unreal to him. Fire ants were swarming in chestnut
cabinets, the island where D would eat cold Spaghet-
tiOs from the can with his hands, where he gave the
boy endless carpet burns, and where they cuddled as
they watched cartoons together. He glided through the
backyard door and noticed that an unused playground
had been built, and to his surprise, Riley's corpse had
been left behind. Despite the body being preserved,
the hole was still there, but as soon as he jammed an
index finger into it, insects rapidly swarmed his body
and began to harvest his flesh. 'Yes, this is how it
should be,' Riley thought. 'Don't throw me in the in-
cinerator. G-d, please allow me the pleasure to haunt
this family forever.'

A boy was glowing as neon green slime danced in a
lava lamp on the nightstand beside him. He dreamed
of Saturn again, his spaceship landing on Titan, asleep
on the rings, his guardian angels at the planet's center. As the spirit caressed his face with skeletal hands,
the tranquil dream switched to a different reel, where
he found the boy holding a silver pistol with the tip
pointed at his forehead. He didn't even check to see
if it had been loaded. People shoot themselves on TV
and come back to life as different characters all the
time. Riley screamed in shock, racing over to yank the
weapon out of the child's hands, and for a moment,
he thought about slapping him across his baby face.
Instead, he rushed to kiss each side of his cheeks before pressing his lips o D's as if to glue them together

permanently. His face was a storm drain of tears, overflowing. In desperation, the words spilled out in dumbfounded fear, "Please don't ever do that again. Do you know what would have happened if you shot yourself? This life isn't a movie. If you did that... Don't ever do that again."

The gun was pressed against the back of D's neck as Riley squeezed him tightly. As he smothered the boy in his tears, a river of blood gushed from a hole in Riley's head.

A

LIGHT

Trauma doesn't just mean remembering; it's also a poison that causes you to forget incremental things. Like hot sand from a Galveston beach drifting from a child's hands. Somehow, a memory appears like a hidden tumor, and I've been consumed again by the time I've located it. I ask you to clarify so that I know that it's real. What more have you hidden from me? Help me unearth myself.

Do you not remember yourself in this picture? Do you not remember going to the Disney theme park in Orlando when you were eight, screaming wildly and holding my hand as we felt our bodies lift out of our seats at the drop in the Tower of Terror ride? He doesn't remember anything anymore. Remember? You had the most adorable smile back then. When you were a little boy, You used to love sea turtles and had a plush doll of one that you carried around with you everywhere. Of course you don't remember. You were too young. But I remember the confusion of being alone in the mall's bathroom and unable to figure out where my underwear went. *You used to make VHS tapes of Yu-Gi-Oh, Dragon Ball Z, and Courage the Cowardly Dog episodes. There's no way you've forgotten your favorite episodes, like when Eustace went to chop down the talking tree. Don't you remember how upset you were that your parents wouldn't buy you a Danny Phantom costume from eBay? The trauma erased everything, didn't it? I wish you could remember—just a few good things.*

And suddenly, a decade and a half later, I remember everything. But the bad is still there, and it's so bad, so ugly, that I'd rather go back to not remembering anything. That boy is dead to me now.

X   X   X

Mother and I took our time moving through the sculpture gallery. She read to me the title of every piece, the artists, the story behind them if there were one, and the materials used to make them. We moved as slow as the immovable art itself and carefully as if our footsteps could shatter stone. When an artwork touched her, we'd sit down on a bench together, and she'd have me lay in her lap so that she could comb my hair with her fingers as she meditated on the piece. A concrete face bent like it had been half-ran over by a train stared back at us. Mother told me what she saw within it as if she were the art curator, having sculpted it with her own hands, or as if the face were her own.

"Not all of us survived." She exhaled fragments of an incomplete novel from her lips. "My grandma, your great-grandma, was only an infant, but she was almost thrown off the boat when our family was traveling to immigrate to America. Many Jews were sent back. Some of our family didn't leave their homes. Those were called shtetls - like the small towns you see when visiting your grandparents in Iowa. Nazis would march them to an open field near the forest, have them dig their own mass grave, and then shoot them in the back of the head, one by one, including the children and infants. If you were to go back to that village, you wouldn't find any Jewish homes or the synagogue, not even the bodies. The cemetery was desecrated, and tombstones were used for sidewalks or wells. Like our history, everything we owned was destroyed or taken by those that sold us to our deaths. Then we came here, to this country, but the community that we tried to build, like a shtetl, is gone now, too. Mostly everyone left for the city. That's when we all abandoned G-d, including myself. Maybe, by telling you this, I'm hoping to fix that loss because I don't want you to be ashamed of who you are, but you're too young to understand anything I'm saying, anyway."

As she went on, I drifted into the sky, the cement head following me around, and when I closed my eyes, a constellation of stars carefully glided me down into a field of long grass. Rain violently poured down on me as if to swallow and consume the pasture. A train on the hill up above passed me by. A woman jumped out of one of the train carts, but she was swept up by the wind, which yanked her under iron wheels that crushed her face in half.

Further inside the vision or dream, I returned to the body of one of my past lives, where I rested on top of a bale with a single straw of hay hanging from my mouth. I gazed at the milky way, made wishes on shooting stars, placed my thumb over the moon as if to consume it, and searched for the Gemini constellation, but I couldn't find it within the glowing soup in the sky. Someone inside the farmhouse was banging on piano keys. It made me want to throw my clarinet into the cornfields and never play music again.

X X X

D enters the tiny witness surveillance room. In this instant, he's twenty-six years old, but still trapped in the body of a dead child. He turns his face to the left and stares confusedly at the painted smiling children frolicking in flower gardens. There's even a set of play toys in a basket. *Am I supposed to take a doll and point at its privates? Do I thrust a finger into the butt part? Why does she need to ask me questions if nothing is going to*

happen to him? Everything has already happened to him. Ev-
erything has already happened to me.

Behind the woman interviewing him, there's a camera locked into a glass case recording them. Somewhere in the facility, an officer, a therapist, and another forensic interviewer watch the footage as it is being recorded. He is fortunate because it wasn't always like this; this will be the only time he will have to answer questions on this subject for legal purposes.

A light above his eyes glides from left to right. Right to left. Left to right. Left to right. Before the woman speaks, he can already hear the sound of snapped glowsticks, pop rocks fizzing on the tongue, the echo of basketballs in a gymnasium, and mid-2000s rap and R&B blasting on the dance floor. She guides him with a calming whisper, "Think back as early as you can. Before the mall incident. Locate the earliest memory you can of feeling safe; somewhere you felt genuinely happy."

X   X   X

The Kroger grocery store had a drop-off for little kids so parents could shop without having their kids running through the aisles. When mom left me there, I'd glue myself to the *A Bugs Life* game on Nintendo 64, which is still the most challenging fucking game I've ever played, its soundtrack sometimes following me even to this day. It makes me think of artificial grass, karate lessons, and pink lemonade. I also see Grandma and Grandpa's house in Iowa, desolate from the world, from its own city, street, and hidden behind the trees. A piece of my flesh was buried in the front yard with a seed, and now the tree is as tall as the house. When I am dead, that tree will be my ladder to heaven. Inside the pith, through ironclad roots, dirt that gives birth, a bridge of white light from Iowa to Poland. That is where all my souls, from the past and now, are held.

X   X   X

My hometown is being transformed into luxury shopping containers. A fading memory. It's too late. Falling rain. Those brief moments of happiness we had as children at great-grandma's farm, picking tomato plants, and eating fresh cherries all seem unreal given everything that's happened to us now. Is this death? This is what I really wanted? This body? At this time? Can I start over again? Hey mom, is it okay if I spend the night at J's for the weekend? Okay! Thanks, ma. Ever since I was a kid, I have wanted to be someone's pet python. Hi. I'm D. Nice to meet you. Oh, cool. Where ya' from? Oh, I'm sorry. I heard all about the storm on the news and from my parents. I'm glad that you're okay and safe and alive. Is your family okay? Like, nobody was hurt? I hope you can find a home soon. Do you like it here so far? I'll be your friend. And I'm sure you'll make a ton while you're here. I wish it were always a sunrise in the autumn, that my body was transparent, and instead of speaking, my voice was a vibraphone. Don't look at him. Stop it. Fuck, he's so sexy. I wonder what he looks like naked. It's not fair. I know he's straight. There's no way. Everyone is straight. I'm such a freak. I shouldn't be looking at a friend like this. If he knew, he wouldn't be so nice to me. I want to know his everything. Not just his body, but what he's thinking about at night. What his home life is like. What scares him most. If he had been touched as a kid like me. What if he already knows, and I'm too scared to do anything, but he's already forgiven me? You're going to turn ugly and go insane when you get older, and your parents will think you're a burden, but maybe, you could just show me your everything, and I could make it alright. I wonder if we'll ever see each other again after this. I'm writing this inside a pain box, which encases an obsidian sphere bouncing aimlessly. I've been told that the sphere will shrink over time, but it seems to feed off my decomposing flesh. Only now do I realize that I visited this room when I first tried to take my life. They say there's a way out that doesn't involve death, but I refuse to believe it. Death is easier. If I could bring myself to do this one last act. You said that giving birth to me was what saved you from another suicide attempt. Sorry, don't care. You should have never given birth to me. Peak selfish move. I have no duty to live for anyone, nor do I owe you my tortured existence for the sake of your distorted comfort. People kill themselves, whatever, end of story, moving on. Your love, and Dad's, it felt like being hated for the longest time. I'm sorry, but I can't be like your Oprah Winfrey survivors. Don't be such a hypocrite. It's not like I hate you; I do love you but don't act like you didn't see this coming. It's a miracle it didn't happen any sooner. What other options did I have in life? Time is nonexistent in the aquarium. When I'm there, the other visitors vanish, and I only see the sea otters, jellyfish, and you. I step outside and imagine myself falling into the Pacific Ocean. The jewelry box of Indra's net. My hometown transformed into a soupy lake of cattle blood. My hometown massacred, set on fire, buried under bullets and train tracks. My hometown of gray concrete, rogue angel militia, suburban Raytheon test subjects, warheads under the floorboards, magazines raining in the classroom, a quiet rape under the child's bedsheets. Make my death into some shitty poetry. My hometown a suburban breeding ground for eugenics, genocide, and pro-suicide campaigns. The vice-principal that jerks off to little girls cuts off your faggot pride shirt and throws you into a pit of wooden spikes. My hometown threatened by the supercollider project. A Ghost town submerged under an artificial lake. Once upon a time, deep in the heart of Texas. You've lost your hands, they've cut out your tongue, how will you continue to pray? A weeping fucktard of an angel jumped from the high school rooftop before it was razed to mountains of cow shit. It's been ten years, you drive back home after spitting on it, and it has been swallowed in an ocean of boiling gore. Rain nuclear weapons upon my hometown, pummel it, don't stop until it's erased from the map, ensure that every last fuck evaporates, and keep going until the crater is as deep as Vredefort.

X   X   X

D visualizes primordial baths, bubbling over like lava in a deep cavern, neon lightsaber blue, skeletal wrists thrusting deep into them. The glow imitated a hospital mirror, where the boy slept in quiet rooms and fish tanks with security cameras beaming red dots on him.

"Force your hands deeper," the therapist instructs from her computer chair. "Negate the colors. You're starting with a fresh sheet of paper. Who's there with you?"

The sea became an oily watercolor painting of misty baby blue and mossy green where he saw multiple faces in one, liquefying and leaving behind many blank pages in a thick sketchbook. D's mind began to draw a field of soybeans, then two boys sitting beside one another, one gazing toward him, while he looked forward at the light that brought the image to life.

It wasn't Riley, nor was it his recently deceased lover, who the therapist immediately theorized. D felt a guilty anger pent up in his gut that he wanted to release, but he wasn't sure the room was a safe enough space for it.

Both boys were made of charcoal lines and were separate shades of beige. Evan took the grass out of his mouth, while tears welted in D's eyes. The brown-haired boy rubbed his cross necklace and apologized with a faint smile, "I'm sorry that I can't be what you want me to be and that what we did together can't be what you want. You want it to last beyond a lifetime. But I can't give that to you. My parents, G-d, even myself, I can't... You know it's wrong, right?"

Obnoxious chunks of snot popped out of D's nostrils as he sobbed and bashed his forehead with his fists. He argued, "But can't we at least remain friends?"

Evan kept smiling as his caramel shirt shook in the warm breeze.

"Not a kid anymore. I can't go back." D spoke, shaking his head as he flipped through the sketchbook. An image of him and J sharing ice cream and wearing matching Digimon shirts. Of him and Evan nuzzled shoulder to shoulder on that hill and that stupid fucking cross necklace and bigoted parents never existing. Another picture drawn with crayons of him and Evan diving into a foam pit on his birthday. The pictures mom and dad took of him, Evan, J, Jasmine, and Sterling, behind Star Wars Episode 1 decorations. Of those deleted pictures that he took of him and his first true boyfriend because he was ashamed of being a faggot, then his boyfriend was dead as fuck, and disintegrating from the world, into the ether, or nothingness.

Venturing off topic, or so it seemed to him, he went on, "You know, when I was in elementary and middle school, sometimes I'd get so anxious that I'd eat sheets of notebook paper. I'd bite my nails until they bled. Eat crayon boxes. The eraser from pencil. Chapstick."

He shuts his eyes as if to staple them closed and hide the light as much as he could, and then relays to his therapist, "You think your pain could have meaning, but I promise it doesn't. Suffering with no meaning or worth. I no longer want to hold onto false senses of security in anyone or put my faith in hollow concepts. I'll keep my heart closed for the rest of my life if I have to."

The light burns a hole through his retinas. Right to left and left to right. As it moves faster, the memories reel slower, and color transforms to sepia and monochrome. With another whisper, the therapist asks,

"Why are you crying?"

His eyes gaze away from her and the camera, through the children painted on the wall, into a mirror reflecting a different figure. Globs of neon green from lava lamps swirled around in his eyes. Being with Riley in bed, touched so gracefully, felt so good, but now, the magnetic forces between him and others felt like moldy slime, cobwebs, and a million threats. In the interviewing room, time is nonexistent, and the woman waited patiently, knowing that the longer you allow someone to dwell in silence, the more the thoughts will canker and consume.

"There's a ghost living inside of me, and I think I'm going to be haunted by it forever."

As soon as the last word escapes his mouth, she immediately responds like an auditory hallucination. Like the static creature living inside of the TV. She changes the subject by interrogating, "What is it that you want to be more than anything?"

"The purest angel. But they don't exist, do they? My parents don't believe in them or G-d." He removes his black yarmulke and squeezes it. "Vampires exist, though."

"Was Riley the vampire?"

"There are others, too. Like me. He made me into one. But you're all monsters, too. It's because of you that he's not here to protect me anymore. None of you will ever understand."

It was as if she saw him as a ball of yarn with a million knots that she could untangle and fix, but each time she tried, the string became thinner or split into smaller pieces. The only way to put together the torn-apart fragments would be to tie more knots. Each question brought more confusion and contradictions. "Maybe it's you that doesn't understand yet." She tied one piece of the string from the end to the middle, then tightened three knots upon each other. The ball of yarn was tangled around him. "He didn't love you. What he did wasn't love. Do you understand that adults aren't supposed to do those things with children?"

His parents loved him but did nothing; they rarely spoke to him and were never around. Riley didn't love him, but he gave him gifts and held him all the time. Love must be absence, betrayal, and sacrifice. Love as magnetic distortion. What if they all loved him? What if none of them did? Does it really matter? Does love matter if it doesn't save the people you care for from hurt and death?

"If I could go back, I'd make sure I had done it right," he muttered, hiding his face from the dancing lights, like snowfall in Iowa, that made him feel more trapped than anything else. "The suicide attempt, I mean. It would have been best if I could have died right then and there. Or I would have liked to have been killed because that's what I think I deserve. If your childhood is taken from you, I think it ruins the rest of your life. You can't get it back. There's nothing I want more than to start over... To be an innocent. Fucking. Child. FOREVER. I want to live in that fantasy and eventually lose my innocence on my own twisted terms -- not the way it fucking... So that's why I wish I were dead."

She leaned over and handed him a set of Polaroids. It was her way of saying that if he had died right then and there, these are the things he would have never witnessed, and as painful and ugly as life can be, he could continue to experience glimpses of happiness he never believed possible. He turned them over and tossed them into the basket of kids' toys before arguing, "But all of these things that you see as blessings came with their own cancer. That sister that I held the day she was born, I never got to see her grow up because I was too dangerous to keep in the house. That guy right there - he's brain dead now. He doesn't even remember who I am anymore. And him? We were going to get married. Jon was my everything, my only sense of hope, and now he's dead. I've seen and felt enough to know that whatever might come in the future isn't worth it. None of this bullshit existence added up to mean anything, so yes, I wish I had died back then. There was never any hope."

The beaming red light from the camera vanished. He was worthless evidence on a tape for her to review later. D was still tied up from memories he couldn't manipulate. As he was attempting to free himself, she stood from her chair, flicked a switch, and left him in the room to vanish into the abyss, the place where kids played with dolls and stuffed animals and plastic rings to chew on while they'd explain to a stranger each part of their body that had been violated. All the lights in heaven shattered and exploded into black holes that eviscerated the angels, and the sun became a frozen dark orb, unable to shed its light anymore.

COME

OCTOBER

While waiting in line to buy candy, D traded a few of his rubber gel bracelets for extra cash, specifically those that felt too gay. He always knew to keep the breast cancer awareness one that said 'I LIKE BOOBS' because it felt like straight armor to him. A girl in front of him even complimented him on his Halloween costume, which he put together himself. Finally, he was Danny Phantom, the cartoon character he masturbated to weekly. JT's brother was working the snack bar, and since they knew each other well, he even handed D a few extra snacks.

He rushed to the dance room, where another one of Missy Elliott's hit songs was playing so loud that D couldn't hear himself. After handing JT a bag of skittles, he stood back and watched as some white boys he knew tried to impress black and Latino girls with their attempts at breakdancing. There wasn't much to do but blush and laugh. Girls kept giving him that stare, but he couldn't figure out how to reciprocate it. Someone told him to dance, and he shrugged it off, then the same person told him to do something useful and ask the DJ to play Get Low by Lil Jon & The East Side Boyz. D did as obliged, but only in the hope of finding other friends along the way that wouldn't embarrass him.

The Kids Night Out dance floor went ballistic as the DJ accidentally played the dirty version of Petey Pablo's Freek-A-Leek. D patiently waited for an opening among the pre-teens shouting and grinding themselves against each other. Once his song request was approved, he sat on the floor beside one of the windows and felt himself panting, ears ringing, skin melting into the floor.

"You okay, D?" Two of his friends from school were knelt down and across from him. Their faces conjoined into something out of a body horror movie. "Where the heck were you? We were waiting in the gym forever." His tongue slid between his words as he tried mumbling his thoughts, but nothing came out. Then a wonky synth blared with Lil Jon's voice as people screamed each line in unison. "Forget it, Sterling. He left us for his white friends. They must have gotten him high or something."

D whined and reached for Jasmine's arm. She helped him up, and the two guided him to the game room, where they could sit him down, far away from the noise. He thought it might have been all the sugar, but it never made him hallucinate or feel like he could cut a hole in the air and crawl through it. Sterling sat with him for a bit longer, waited for him to finish a water bottle, and then followed him to the bathroom, where D could do nothing but stare at his distorted reflection in the mirror.

"Bloody Mary… Bloody Mary… Bloody Mary. I'm… going ghost!"

Riley was inside the glass, his head held up to heaven, dry blood caked to his button-up, and his body swirled as if he were in a drunken daze. He was supposed to be dead, D was learning to hate him, and then he had the nerve to haunt him like this. The boy felt himself sucked into the glass until his forehead was against it, bridging into Riley's hollow chest. It was the comfort that he sought in every nightmare. It was milky tea, it was a squeezed raw tomato, it was the skin in his mouth that he bit, like swallowing hard, blackberries crushed in a copper cup, sticky and and thick.

When Riley encased him in the tomb of his withering arms, the boy pulled back and screamed, the limbs falling down with him. It was dust in his mouth from licking a tombstone on a double dare, it was hiding in a gun safe, it was hiding behind curtains in the sunlight, it was a rusty nail through a bone in the neck.

The friend D had been ignoring all month helped him catch his breath by dragging him until his back was pressed against a toilet stall. Sterling couldn't see it, but while D's mouth was drooped open, he vomited ectoplasm that looked like fuzzy cotton candy, which evaporated as it rose in the air. Once he was back on his feet with his frail skinny legs wobbling, he thought about crying, succumbing to rage and grief, but he knew he couldn't. It's not something his friend would understand, and it would only disturb him more. All he could do was apologize, hope that he would someday forget, and spend the rest of the night shooting hoops in the gymnasium with him. And that could be their forever – the end.

X   X   X

Riley was living inside an RPG adventure game, trapped within a gothic cathedral, sweaty fingers attempting to find a home in the bricks of the arch as his legs dangled between a pier. A golden cross fell from his left pocket. The more pixelated his body became, the harder it was for him to hold on. Behind closed eyelids was a simulated jungle or a rainbow of different colored pipes forming and vanishing in all directions, screensaver worlds that hid pornography, his true self. At the very bottom, where he knew he'd eventually land and explode into a mess of gore, was a boy reaching to catch him. A gun fell from his right pocket, then VHS tapes, a PS2 controller, a CD player, and an alligator skull. "Oh G-d, oh no, please don't let me go, G-d, I don't want to fall, oh no!" The sound of a cape of wind eddied around him as he let go, fell through the concrete, and kept falling through the earth as his dead ghost form descended rapidly into hell. Maybe the boy he loved would eventually die and catch up to him at some point along the way. This narcissistic delusion that would inevitably become a reality comforted him as his soul became boundless and eventually stretched far enough to make a diseased womb out of the universe.

X   X   X

A six-flags commercial featuring Vengaboys' "We Like to Party" was fighting through the static on a boom-box in the arcade room while a group of ten-year-old boys gathered around a foosball table. D stopped a shot with his goalie, and with a quick flick of his palm, he remained an undefeated champion. The other boys were inquiring about a dare that JT came up with; he challenged that whoever had the guts to say Bloody Mary three times in the bathroom with the lights off could get drunk with him and his older brother over the weekend. One of the boys instilled fear in the others, lying that he knew someone that had their eyes plucked out after saying it. When another kid called him out, the word faggot was thrown around, then pussy ass faggot, because nobody was willing to do it.

"Bloody Mary is real," D stated as he stared at the

others. "I've seen her at J's place. She doesn't hurt me, though. But it's true that she has plucked eyes out of people's sockets and used them for herself. She does that to see the fear in you with your own eyes before she kills you. I'll do it, but I don't think any of you should. I think she likes me."

The others silently watched as D went to the restroom and carefully shut the door. In the darkness, he felt his skin emanating a dim, pearly glow that lit the dense piss-scented space around him. Someone from out-side banged on the door as if to try and make him shriek, but he expected someone to do that. With his eyes wide open, patiently waiting for them to be removed, he spoke into the mirror, "Bloody Mary, Bloody Mary, Bloody Mary." Nothing happened, so he repeated it louder.

It's not like he expected anything to happen since he made up everything he said to the others. However, he remained in the bathroom, mumbling to himself in the hope that they could hear so that he could tell them about a conversation he had with Bloody Mary. He thought about how he and Evan had touched and sucked each other's dicks at this daycare. The more he thought about it, the further away Evan was, and the more disgusted he felt because he wanted it, or anyone, to touch him like that again. A feeling over-took him, like being entrapped in a straitjacket, and his shoulders and the back of his head jolted against the wall while his crotch thrust outward. He gritted his teeth, stretched his lips, and pressed his nails as hard as possible into his pubis. When the tension and pain were too much, he instantly returned to his senses and flicked the switch. An ebony figure made of smoke stood near the toilet and reached for him. The second he saw it, he twisted the doorknob, threw himself onto the ground to escape it, and tried to keep his cool while the others surrounded him. All the kids, except JT, were just as disturbed by the horror nailed to D's face.

D thought about something his father once said to him when he had woken up, thinking someone had tried to knock over his dresser. "There's no evidence of ghosts being real. What you thought you saw was just chemicals in your brain sparking because you were scared. You formed the image you wanted to see based on your own fears. When people die, they don't come back. They don't go to heaven, they don't go to hell, and nobody's soul is trapped here. Nothing happens after you're dead. You don't need to be scared of dead people hurting you anymore."

Trauma was more than a memory, nightmare, or flashes of dissociation. It was also the constant hallucinations that felt as real as anyone else's presence. His eyes might as well have been removed the day he had first been raped. If there was no redemption or way of being an angelic virgin in heaven, he might as well be dead. Vampires aren't real. Ghosts aren't real. A boy with bloody underwear, the corpse he kissed, screaming into a pillow in a hospital bed after a suicide attempt, all too real.

♫ ♫ ♫

We like to party. We like. We like to party.

♫ ♫ ♫

Every house in the neighborhood was lathered in decorations, with carved pumpkins on every doorstep, orange and purple lights in the bushes, stickers of skeletons and Frankenstein on the windows, fake bioluminescent spiderwebs ebbed around like cotton candy in the trees, and inflatable monsters in the yard. A week ago, D and his father built a coffin out of wood in the garage, spray-painted it black, and placed an animatronic skeleton inside of it that would pop up, scream, and frighten anyone hoping to get a fistful of candy. It wasn't the scariest house, but he was proud of it. Nothing made him happier than to see kids sobbing when they saw a clown with LEDs in its eyes hanging from the front door.

As they pulled up to the garage, D thought about how Riley would sit out in the driveway with the candy bowl that had a talking goblin hand inside of it. The hand would repeat with a glitchy hoarse croak, "Waaaaaaant some candy? He ha ha ha ha." Dressed in an all-black robe that veiled most of his face, he'd let a child stick their hand in the bowl, which he placed against his crotch, and then shout, "BOO!" When the child would scream, D would squeeze a plastic heart in his hand, which made his skeleton mask fill with fake blood.

Halloween is a day when violence and death are joyously celebrated. The fictional and inhuman come to life, and nobody is ashamed to take these roles within a costume for a day. People seek out attractions that will disturb them the most, while others are permitted to get off on scaring others. It's also a day of cartoon specials, sorting candy on the carpet, roasting pump-kin seeds, freshly baked sugar cookies, the perfect au-tumn day where nature's rot imitates the decorations, all before winter paralyzes and religious holidays re-decorate the yards.

Once D made it into his room, he yanked a cord from behind his dresser, wrapped a pair of Halloween lights around his bed, and looped his neck with it. Miniature purple ghosts were pressing into his throat and gnar-ring at him. "Bloody Mary…" He squeezed tight and felt his eyes bulge. "Fucking, Bloody Mary." It was too strenuous to repeat. His brain wouldn't let him fill his vision up with any more stardust and forced him to surrender. A moment later, he dug his nails into the scabs around his pubis, hoping to draw more blood to taste, and then his mother opened the door, unsure who was in her son's bed anymore.

X   X   X

JT wanted to be the next Eminem, a white ten-year-old rapper boy with a shaved head, tall and impover-ished to the bones, playground freestylist, lyrics about stabbing his mother, a failure at every subject in fifth grade, clinging to his deranged sixteen-year-old broth-er that he'd never measure up to. Nobody could throw down like him in a rap battle or pencil tapping contest or beatbox like his drum machine of a mouth.

50 Cent's '*In Da Club*' was cranked up, eating the van's speakers as the kids inside recited the lyrics togeth-er, imagining big-breasted women were at their feet, attaching golden charms to their ankles and fingers.

In a few days, it would be JT's birthday; D felt special knowing he'd be at his side all weekend to celebrate it. As soon as they were let out of the van in front of the mall, JT's older brother, Austin, took D in a chokehold until he started squirming fearfully. "Chill fag, just playing with you," Austin grunted, pushing him out of the way and to his friend. JT was laughing along, jumping; it's cool to get beaten up because that's what men do. Yet, faggot D rubbed the sore ring around his neck and held back tears. Austin's friend, Sam, was also with them and snarled in his Korn shirt and baggy black pants. He towered over D as he teased him, "Where'd you get that Pink Floyd shirt, anyway? Target? Pink Floyd's for fucking faggots. They even have a gay ass rainbow on an album cover. Take that shirt off before someone beats you up or thinks we're gay, too. Does your mom make you wear those retarded fucking cowboy boots, too? You're a redneck, faggot, and a Jew. Why are you friends with this gay ass kike, JT? Are you two sucking each other's dicks or some shit? You're not gay, too, are you?"

"Fuck you. I'm not gay." JT held his friend back. "D's not gay either. You're the faggot! Korn is fucking gay as fuck! That dude sings about his dad fucking him and shit, and he sings like a fucking gaywad, too."

"Didn't your dad rape your ass? So what does that make you, queer?" Sam stuck a chunk of cancer beneath his back teeth and spat at the kid's shoes. "You think you're cool? You don't even have hair on your dick. Talk shit when you can get pussy, faggot."

In the spur of the moment, JT tried to fight him by punching with the side of his palms, which went on until Austin finished a cigarette and pulled them apart. Sam stood still, held ground, twice as tall as the skinhead kid, and kept egging him on the whole time. Then they walked into the Dicks sporting goods store and went their separate ways.

"Your brother and his friend are sort of assholes," D remarked. As they stood alone in front of ammunition boxes, he quietly asked, "Did your dad really rape you? Is that why your parents are divorced?"

Immediately, JT refuted, "No... Sam's just an asshole. They broke up because my mom's a slut. She's already trying to marry this new guy... I wish they were both dead. Dad, too. Then we can get all his money, and I can live with my rich-ass grandparents in California."

Somewhere upstairs, D's mother was working, selling expensive handbags after she had quit selling lingerie. He thought about sprinting upstairs to surprise her, then he and his friend could ice skate or win ten or fifteen packs of fun dip at Dave and Buster's. The thought became an insurgent trance in which his mind melted into the mall's structure. He imagined his brain as the cotton stuffing in the Build-A-Bear workshop, a body slamming into a toilet stall, his limbs as dirty sticky escalators, a voyeuristic predator chewing on the end of a table in the food court. When he came out of the vision, his friend was gone. Instead, it was Sam and Austin that were juxtaposed with him.

It was common for people to name their children after places in Texas. Austin, Dallas, McKinney, Houston, Tyler, Denton. Austin was just that, the *keep Austin weird*, and his tastes were too obscure to fit the mall-goths that lurked around from Hot Topic to Barnes and Noble. He wore his hair long and wavy like that of a death metal musician and showed off his unique music taste with black band tank-tops that displayed his sinewy triceps. Sam was a greasier and uglier version of Austin, who had to make up for his cliched appearance by attempting to be just as tough and vile.

Austin reached for D with one hand, squeezed his shoulder, and brought him closer to his chest. "JT says you don't get scared easily. So how about this... Does this scare you at all?" He twisted the boy around so that D was pinned to him, revealed a hunting knife, and let the light glimmer off it and into D's eyes. Slick, sharp, well oiled, the handle wobbled as if used countless times before. "Scared now? Am I scarier than Bloody Mary?"

While Austin dangled the blade around in D's face, Sam made sure nobody was in the aisle of the already desolated store before he held out a pistol toward the kid. It was the knife that brought D into a panic. His legs buckled, and as much as he tried to scream, his voice wouldn't let him. He dry heaved and felt the black dots froth in his eyes while his skin sizzled from being touched. A fist full of scorpions shoved into his cum filled mouth. A vampire is thrust out into the sunlight. An angel caught being dressed as the morning star.

"If you scream, run, or tell anyone, we'll fucking kill you. We'll cut you to fucking pieces. Nobody would even give a shit if you were dead. You're just a stupid faggot, anyway."

G-d must have defeated whatever curse Riley had on him and the world for a second because he managed to break from Austin's deadly embrace and sprint away. He thought about hiding inside a canoe, under a rack with cowboy boots, but with them too close, he didn't want to risk it. Instead, he trapped himself inside a rifle storage cabinet, one of a dozen lined up in an aisle near a restroom.

"Please, G-d, please help me. I'm sorry. I know I should have said something. I'm an idiot. I know. I'm sorry. It's my fault. Don't let them hurt me. I don't want to be hurt again."

From outside the container, there was the sound of toilets flushing, piss streams, and parents helping their children. He sunk into a sphere as he listened intently and tried to remember. Why did he want to remember? What peace would it bring if he knew what the stranger had looked like? He had always wondered what the man wanted with his underwear, if he kept it, and what he did with it. D imagined looking down on himself in a public bathroom, comfortably asleep and underneath a sink. Then there was silence like there had been before he was found. Hundreds of hands emerged from the floor, walls, and ceiling to grab them both, to rip their bodies apart with piercing chains, machetes, kitchen knives, and revved-up chainsaws.

More than an hour passed before D left the safe and wandered around the store until he found JT. Austin and Sam were with him, and they all acted ashamed of what they had done and shocked that he had hidden for so long. Austin spoke in a higher note as if calming down a baby and construed, "Hey man... It was just a joke. We were just fucking with you. You're cool, D. We like you. If you're friends with JT, then you're our friend, too. That should make you proud, man. You're with the coolest now."

X   X   X

A vampire without a face or any sense of recogniz-
able skin shapeshifted from a bat and into a mist that
lurked from a centimeter of open space in a toilet
stall—peeking, preying, touching itself, sucking up
slobber and snot into a hole filled with insects. It waited patiently for the perfect opportunity to strike and
cleave; a child, not just any child, but a lost one that's
also very young and alone, a total silence of nobody
else entering anytime soon, no sound except a trickle
of piss.

The boy tried peeing in at the urinal, but couldn't do it
in front of someone, so he went into a stall and tried
again. Kid felt dizzy and like time was moving too fast.
Too hot in Texas, scorched Earth. D always nervous
around adults, how they slam doors and scream while
pointing knives at each other. His eyes were security
cameras flickering through every back hallway where
customers weren't allowed. Security guards, employees taking out the trash, kicking cardboard boxes, sobbing while smoking a cigarette, a nest of semen and
venom bubbling like an oily swamp.

"Cute doll," The man commented. He glided closer
to the kid, who held his hazelnut stuffed Build-a-Bear
bear to his chest, almost as if it would protect him if
he could thrust it into his heart. "Can I touch it? Can I
play with it?" Those words might not be what the man
said; it could have been something Riley whispered to
him in his bed a year later, phrases that meshed to-

-gether as years went on. It didn't matter what visions his brain constructed for him to cope.

X   X   X

"You gotta take it all off, dude."

As he veered over the snapped tree stump and gazed into the natural pool that fed into Blanco River, translucent frogs climbed from his toes and up to his tanned belly. After he took off his underwear, he held it in both hands, imagining that it was the stranger holding them or the blood spot he'd find when changing the following day after Riley raped him. Raped. The new word that confiscated every thought. Not laid, not sex, not a fuck. His briefs were red like the blood he always saw, and he thought about tasting the fabric to see if it was actually blood but remembered they were staring up at him, waiting to see him dive. He barely knew how to swim and was sure they'd try to push him under like everyone enjoyed doing to him, but he couldn't pussy out now. That would be faggot shit.

His black yarmulke was the last to come off. Something he'd leave behind for the bats and owls and moonlight fairies. Arms spread out wide. And then he let himself fall forward.

The frogs danced from the water and into hogweed as he came up and choked on memories of drowning. His thin arms wobbled as he panicked to hold himself up from a drop that descended into sunken caves. What surprised him most was when Austin helped to hold him up and calmly taught him how to float on his back. He reminded him two times, with one hand on his back, "Just relax like you're dead. Relax like you're dead. See? Gotta chill out more often, man."

Just relax like you're dead. Relax like you're dead. Like you're dead. You're dead. Like you're dead. You're dead. Dead.

Skin turned to soil and ash. Like water balloons thrown around and exploding on the last day of elementary school. The taste of sucking on a patriotic ice pop, gums splintered by the wooden stick. Limbs snapped apart like melting fun pops. A sun was sliced into four by ancient trees. The polluted sky hid wreckage of an exploded space shuttle. D imagined dead astronauts hanging by their feet from branches, taking one of their spacesuits, and venturing from Saturn to the heart of the Scorpion Nebula. Luscious purple spheres radiated in his mouth, and a deluge of voids painted over his mossy green eyes.

Toes in mud and worm guts. Specs of dirt on a cigarette. JT lit one for himself, handed another to D, and was impressed that he didn't have to show him how to smoke it. His uncles taught him last summer, just as their father had taught them while they were kids on the farm. As the boys smoked, Austin and Sam shared a bottle of liquor. While they dressed, D had done his best not to stare at anyone's asses or cocks, to play it straight as possible, and squinted at the irony of how gay all of this felt to him.

After they were all dressed, Austin made a pipe out of a soda can and began passing it around. D remembered when he smoked weed for the first time with two of his uncles and thought it would kill him. The teenagers upraised him as he took a second hit like a champ. "Fuck yeah, this kid knows how to smoke." "Damn, your family smoked you out at ten years old? Isn't that child abuse?" "You're gonna be such a druggie when you reach our age." "Man, this kid is fucked."

One of the translucent frogs had returned to D. He reached down to grasp it and cupped his palms. Its pea-sized heart beat rapidly and reminded him of the tic of his father's pacemaker, or an acrylic painting of internal organs he'd seen at a museum with his mother. There was too much fragility contained in the idea of this amphibian, which made the traumatized Jew regard all of the ugliness and tragedy he'd seen and heard. In the eyes of the creature, he saw his ancestors taken from their shtetl, digging their own graves, and being shot to death. He saw the band of Klan members protesting out of a rural synagogue in Iowa. Riley's head cracked apart from a gunshot wound and sucking him in through the hole. When it jumped from his hands, he then realized it hadn't been translucent at all. Another hallucination. It leaped toward Sam and was crushed under the visceral slam of his heel.

"Holy shit, dude," Austin wowed over as his friend scraped the guts off his foot. "You're fuckin' sick, man."

"What? Killing shit is cool. Have you ever eaten frog legs? What's the difference?"

"You just shouldn't do that shit in front of them."

Sam looked the two of us over like we were cows hanging from our feet and about to have our stomachs split open. He continued to stare and went on, "Fuck them. I'd kill them too. Kill anyone, everyone. Everybody deserves to die." The two boys didn't flinch when he attempted to scare them with a bellowed scream. It's as if they had already been desensitized down to the core. The only thing left for them to experience was their own deaths. JT wanted to live forever, and being raised a Catholic, he knew that he'd at least find peace in Heaven. D didn't care at all. He was ready to die with everything in him, even on days as hypnagogic as these.

On the way back home to Dallas, with one Eminem CD playing after the other, Sam randomly twisted back from his seat and silently dug his eyes into D's for what felt like a lifetime. He stared as if he had seen the most beautiful sunrise. It was a look D had seen too many times before and made his stomach churn. Texas must have been infested with vampires. And then Sam winked. The two never made eye contact again for the rest of the night.

X   X   X

JT's mother worked at a barbershop and cut D's hair once a month. D's mom became good friends with her, whispering about their children's trauma, their plans to make more money, house parties to sell Halloween candles, plans to take the kids to Houston or Austin, and the feeling of never being a good enough parent. Since JT's mom knew about him more than the other adults, D often wondered if her gaze into him was different. Most parents would never allow a raped kid to hang out with their children, but she brought him into her debilitated family as if he were a wounded feral dog.

D was handed over from out of a car and into a house and into another car, another family, loving and protecting the damaged skeleton child with a metal muzzle over his gnarled mouth. On the ride, he dreamt of a conversation he had with J about being able to enter his past lives vividly. It would happen when he'd fall asleep in class, whenever he had a fever, or when boredom would lead to fear of dissociation. In all these previous existences, there was also another version of Riley there. It's as if they were both born to collide with each other, like a car crash happening in slow motion, like the sun swallowing up the galaxy before it eats itself. In another world, he'd live to experience even more abuse. A glimpse of Saturn hiding behind Earth's moon. But in this life, he saw himself dead. That's why he told J that when he dies, he will be his guardian angel until the universe expires, when all is empty and pure, and everyone is bathed in a radiant infernal heaven.

D woke up and found himself snuggled into the chest of JT's stepfather. He was pressed against the reset of the family and a few strangers inside a wagon, with carved pumpkins at the center and a feathering of hay under their shoes. He'd forgotten that they were even going to this event, something he knew he wouldn't like, but he couldn't pussy out in front of his friends. The first scares were ghouls and clowns, nothing too terrifying for him. While he was lightening up to the haunt, a chainsaw revved behind him and attacked the wagon, raining sparks across his back and neck. He turned around and saw the mask, voiceless throat screaming, and became paralyzed back into the step-

-father's crotch.

For a split second, D imagined the chainsaw man digging into his mother's face and mangling it into a salad of pulverized brains and bone. When it was done with her, a hallucinatory faceless man unloaded an entire magazine into D's face. Bullets entered his eyes, the forehead, the sides an inch above his ears, from under the jaw, from the scalp, so many tiny holes with gushing fountains of blood and light exiting them. Why is it that D thought Riley would be the only one that could save him from this?

Pumpkin lights were strung around trees and led further down the hayride path leading to the haunted house. Above, the violet sky glided like a tape fast-forwarding down over decaying cedar elm. The cart stopped in front of a green alien crucified with barbed wire suffocating and sheathing most of its body. As they stepped out, D glanced into the woods near the parked vehicles and saw a face like that of the Bloody Mary in J's house. It continued to expand, mouth agape and jaw splitting apart until it had consumed the entire forest. Effervescent dead skin flakes rained down over them, but only he noticed it. The face screamed like a pig in a panic that knows it'll soon be killed. Its teeth were like the milky eyes of a dead cow inside the slaughterhouse he visited with his school. Corpse, flesh, death, all over, what else was there to life other than to be tortured, die, and then decay? And here they were, celebrating the spectacle of murder and the unknown. Eventually, they would all be the scarecrow chainsaw man, the crucified alien, the psychotic zombie clown.

Thunderstorm sound effects croaked above them all

as they entered the haunted house. Black plastic bags were taped to the ceiling, and aluminum foil coated the windows. It reminded D of his uncle's meth house, where a killer might have hidden under the floorboards. Fake polyester cobwebs with plastic spiders over a broken staircase. A dead body was hanging from the chandelier. A flicker of lights on a rotting silicone face. The Halloween movie theme song played on cue as the group carefully entered the kitchen. Michael Myers emerged from a closet and acted as if he were about to stab JT in the face, but he stopped at the last second and robotically retraced his steps back to where he came from. This made D remember when he was visiting one of his uncle's apartments, and while he was watching an Alicia Keys music video, he clicked open the other tab that led to the Freddy Versus Jason website. After staring at the two characters' menacing faces on the poster for several minutes, D tried to find his uncle in each room, but to no avail. The longer he searched, the more he became afraid. Of what? His uncle, something else, the nothing, or being left alone. When he returned to the Windows 98 computer, the movie preview was playing, and then his uncle came at him with a machete while wearing the Michael Myers mask. Even though the knife never entered him, his body reacted as if it did; shocks of electricity centered around his chest, screaming bolts of sheer horror until his iced-out uncle tossed the knife aside and hugged him tightly. "It's just a joke," he reassured. "Calm down. You're okay." Everything was a joke. The years of forced sucking, swallowing, and penetration. Dead bodies with bullet holes. And it was all going to be okay, someday.

Michael Myer's sister lay dead over the bed in one of the bedrooms, the murder frenzy stab marks from forehead to pubic area. Glittery fake blood was caked to the sheets, the cracked floorboard, and across the painted-over cardboard walls. Another woman appeared from the mirror, screaming and crying in blissful lunacy. The two teenagers moved back when she got close to them; it was as if only a woman could intimidate them. She took a gun to her head, and an explosive gunshot ricocheted around the room. There she lay dead, and then a door opened. Death as the passage to the next purgatory hole.

Beyond Styrofoam caves, they entered a kaleidoscopic maze, where cold air shot through a hole, carnival music played gently, and strobe lights danced in a maze of mirrors. The group was forced apart by the illusions and people yelling into their faces. D couldn't find any of them anymore. All he could see were feet, his eyes bending into trapezoids, the chainsaw man, the scarecrow, the crucified alien, now an angel, but its face demented and gyrated into a grisly mess. A man in a bloody clown outfit stepped towards him; the negative energy emitting from him jolted D to his knees into prayer, davening, and he begged for it all to stop in his soup of snotty tears.

"Why are you crying?" The clown asked him. "Why are you scared? There's nothing to be afraid of. Do I scare you? Why do I scare you? BOO!!! Hahaha! Do you think I'm scary? That's not so nice. I didn't get to choose what I am. What's so fucking scary? WHAT'S SO FUCKING SCARY?"

An angel blanketed D, and he continued to pray for mercy in its grace, still sobbing until JT's stepfather carried him on his back throughout the rest of the haunted house. With his eyes closed, all he could hear were the screams of everyone else, the hum of fog machines, and the revved-up chainsaw from afar. Toward the end of the attraction, they had to squeeze through a tight plastic tunnel. D opened his eyes, seeing all black, the heavenless world, and then shut his eyes to suck in the womb white pearl world. Here, everything was safe, like in death, where all his lives were intertwined.

When he woke up, he found himself in JT's home, slanted over on the sofa in the darkness, with waves of analog static crashing in all directions on a TV. As he stood up, he tasted the mildew and dust on his tongue from the ancient, dilapidated house and felt as if someone was waiting to jump out and stab him in every direction of the living room. It's as if he never left the haunted house. The clown had comforted him into a grave. He carefully tiptoed to JT's door, nudged it, and it creaked halfway open. His friend was playing Metroid Fusion, entombed in his bedsheets, and was briefly startled when D crept over to him. He sat on the side of the bed to watch the Game Boy screen, where sirens wailed and sea monsters exploded from rocket blasts. After JT had died too many times and didn't know what else to do at the current level, the skinhead kid shut off his game system and nervously rolled his eyes around the room.

"You believe in ghosts, right?" JT asked in the hope of reassurance.

D nodded. He didn't want to talk about the ghost in his best friend's house or how his dead abuser haunted him with his every breath and that it seemed the dead were obsessed with wanting him to join them.

"And you've seen 'em, too, right?"

He nodded again. In his mind, he spoke, 'Don't you see that I am a ghost?'

"Yeah, well, this place is haunted, too. This isn't a joke, either, like some stupid thing my brother and his friend would do. It's seriously haunted. And I think it's been getting worse. Maybe... it's because everything here is getting worse. My mother, my stepdad, just what's been going on. It's like. It's like some negative energy is building, manifesting, taking shape, and consuming everything here. You get that, don't you? My mom... She told me about what happened to you. Your mom told her. My dad, he did some things, and so... I get it. There was someone else, but I can't talk about it. And since that all stopped, this ghost has been attacking me. Her face, it's like rotting intestines or soil and shit mixed together. Sometimes, she asks me to help her or save her. And other times, she sprints straight up to me and screams into my face."

There was a void in the silence that tore a hole through reality. The pit in the stomach, that's where they were imprisoned. It was outside of the bedroom, shapeshifting in the hallway and peeking through the door with a sullen, absent gaze, as if forgetting where it was, who it was, observing these soon-to-be-dead boys.

JT grinned briefly while fidgeting his fingers and continued, "I can still recall the face as if it were right in front of me. Cold dead fish eyes with a pastel glow in the iris, pale wet skin, its lips were all bloody and chewed apart, and its mouth kept expanding as if it were going to eat me. And I could feel it sucking on me. Sucking up my soul. I froze. That terrifying freeze of, I can't do anything, I can't move, I'm gonna die, nobody can save me, I can't protect myself. And then I'd always wake up as if it never happened."

"Yeah," was the only thing D could think to respond. But he felt what he heard deep to his heartless core. "Now I don't want to sleep. I don't know if I could. It's just, I don't want to see it. I don't want it to attack me. So I have to stay awake and be prepared. But then again, if I fell asleep, it could still find a way to enter my dreams."

The door slammed shut, and a trophy fell from JT's dresser. Neither of the boys looked at each other. It's as if they knew that doing so would bring the spirit toward them. Instead, they focused vigilantly on the door, attempting to watch the entire room, believing their brave eyes would protect them. Eventually, they would grow tired and fall asleep together. A haunting, negative energy in the shape of a melting oval would feed off their nightmares and trauma and continue to expand its hateful purpose into the house's plasmic atmosphere. Energy forces like these were growing all over the city every day. Soon, tombstones would be raining over North Dallas and crush them all.

X   X   X

A son will ask his mother, "Why Texas?" There was a rationalization behind the idea, but now it didn't make much sense. *We can make Texas ours. I know it's not the best place, but it's better than where you were born.* There were emotions he couldn't express, even if she could sometimes read through the lines and glimpse behind his moonstone eyes. Like when she caught him rubbing himself while watching *Lady and the Tramp II: Scamp's Adventure*, hypersexualized faggot kid imagining himself as a silver-furred pup humping another pup. Or the instances of antisemitism at school and daycare or on his dad's side of the family. This wasn't the right place to exist as a homosexual or a Jew. It wasn't the place to heal, either. Not that he understood what he was supposed to be recovering from.

She would have him wear cowboy boots with a faux-golden buckle that read 'Deep in the Heart of Texas,' a tucked-in turquoise plaid shirt and a rodeo felt hat. He would hold a baseball in one hand and smile at the camera, pretending to be happy and not thinking about a strange absence emanating around him, a loss for someone gone for good. The camera would blind him, and his parents would frame the picture and put it on a coffee table that would be smashed to pieces when the boy's father exploded into a cataclysmic rage over a shitty Cowboy's football game. Still, the picture would remain in a perfect state, even with the confetti of glass shards over it, and only he would know what was behind that fake, grimy smile.

Worms manifested and squirmed inside his brain. His body felt like sandpaper as she twisted one arm around his neck while the other gripped his hair. No, that was a hug and her massaging his scalp. Why did it make him think of something else? The boulders grew heavier inside of his eyes. Gazing into a cold, sterile nothing, depressive infinity, a carcass bloated up in the river. The sunset was a hemorrhage above his right eye. It was a grape cut in half and spurting plasma in the microwave. A broken nose. Where was mother? She was right there. No, before that. He shouldn't think like that. She's here now, and that's what's supposed to matter.

His mother lived in Texas for several months when she was ten. She lived in a hotel room with her parents and had only one friend, a boy who lived in a trailer park in the parking lot across from her who would walk her to and from school. As she smelled the bubblegum-scented body wash in her son's hair, she recalled walking through the woods with the boy, how they carefully stepped over syringes, avoided making eye contact with people that were homeless, and when they walked in on the boy's mother prostituting herself on the sofa.

Evil was supposed to be over. Riley was gone, but there were still others, and after them, there would be even more. They, too, could become evil over time. Succumb to a virus in the barren crimson air. Deep in the heart of Texas, this land was their land, a purgatory unbirthing itself into hell. Your son will become a drug addict, he will sell dirty pictures of himself to older men, he will have sex with strangers, he will be raped and beaten again, and he will not tell you about this because he's ashamed of what he is, of what you would say, your silence, you have abandoned him, and yet he fears of another form of abandonment. You will find him dancing in a noose, you will see a gash in his wrist, you will see bubbles foaming from his mouth, and you will send him away. His present and future will consist of only being consumed by the past, leading him nowhere but through epileptic streams of trauma. He would have lived this life if you hadn't let him go beforehand. So let him go. Let the child die.

On the front of JT's porch were illuminated decorations of oversized grinning pumpkins and ghosts, a witch filled with cotton on the straw rocking chair, and the shadow of a zombie on a window that led into the kitchen. JT and a cluster of his best friends from daycare and school sat on the stairs carving pumpkins with stencil designs. They'd place piles of guts and seeds on baking trays, which would return to the kitchen, into the oven, and come back as roasted seeds for them to enjoy. Afterward, half of them set up a tent in the backyard, while others prowled the streets as the sunset melted over the centuries-aged and historic homes.

While the others socialized, D hid behind JT's mother as she chain-smoked in the backyard, merging the mobile house phone with her face, flicking ashes that caked into her dyed abalone silver hair. Sirens of thunder roared like a symphony of steel clashing together, yet it remained a feverish ninety degrees, even with the funereal charcoal clouds painting the sky. There were healed scars all over the woman's wrists and arms and shoulders, thick and ritualistic and riveting. When she got off the phone, she turned to D, the only boy wearing a skullcap, and confided, "I was just talking to your mom, actually. About mom things... She's a good woman. She understands. I could learn a lot from her. But maybe it's too late for me."

He didn't know what to say back, but he could feel her shame and dread. JT's mother put out her cigarette before taking him into her arms and rocking him back and forth, doing something to him that his own moth-

-er wasn't allowed to do. If he could, he'd climb into any other mother's womb for shelter, but not his own. Even if she were to disembowel herself and plead mortal guilt, it wouldn't be enough.

"Go and play with the others," she ordered, wiping away makeup and tears against her palms.

The boys out front were sharing stories about the scariest things they'd ever seen, some real and some undoubtedly fabricated. One had seen a UFO up close, and another had escaped an apocalyptic hurricane, one had a broken leg after falling off the monkey bars during recess, and J mentioned the ghost in his house. While D sorted through Halloween masks, one of the boys asked him to share his experience. D held onto an alien mask, felt around the black cloth on the other side, and confessed, "I saw someone shoot themselves in the head in front of me." He paused and stared at the mask until he saw himself as the alien. After slipping it on, he made a fake gun with one hand and pretended to blast the boy across from him. "BLAM! Just kidding."

'I'm not human; I'm an alien,' D thought and convinced himself.

JT and the rest of the boys came up the yard from the side and crouched down to scare some others from behind. They'd been listening for a while. The bald kid snickered, "Saw my mom getting fucked in the ass in the bed right next to me while my brother and I were on vacation in Austin, Texas. That's pretty scary, huh?" Then came the ew's and gross and what the fuck's. Immediately, D's mind recalled the cuts, the cigarette ash, and how tight she gripped him in their embrace.

They played a ping-pong tournament with JT winning it and Super Mario Party 3 on a Nintendo 64 and hide and seek where D hid in Austin's bedroom and nobody dared to go in there so he won and nobody found him and everyone imagined that he just disappeared and JT said the ghosts had taken him and after hiding under the bed with pornographic magazines and a bag of weed and a pipe he stumbled around the room and went through his CD rack of nu-metal cheesy alternative rock post-grunge junk the jewel case breaking apart when he opened them and he felt his fingers over the rough black fabric of Hot Topic band shirts and thought about putting one of them on but when one them fell down he just closed the closet and rested on the bed while listening to feet thumping and shoulders clashing against the walls of narrow hallways and his own feet melted into the vermillion red rug that lead him to a computer chair and then he wobbled the mouse until the dimly lit screen woke up and there was a badly pixelated wallpaper of a crouched crying emo angel boy with torn wings surrounded by icons and virus popups and he went into Internet Explorer and into the history out of curiosity and clicked a link that lead to a video that played for only thirty seconds before a paywall came up two barely eighteen-year-old boys sucking each other off and D closed it out and deleted the days' browser history and shut down the computer and walked away thinking, 'I knew he was gay. He's like me. I wonder if he was raped like JT', and then he went into the dresser because he knew that Austin was staying over at Sam's tonight. As he was pulling back clean underwear that he wanted to smell, he came across a dozen knives and switchblades for hunting, survival, whatev-

-er. So D thought about how his parents would never let him have one, but all the other kids, including J whose parents were devout Christians addicted to Fox News had given him a tactical folding knife. There's no way Austin would notice if one of his many knives went missing, plus, what did he use them for anyway? It's not like he slept with them or checked on them like eggs ready to hatch, so he took a small knife and stuck it halfway into his shorts and hid the rest with his shirt and carefully left the room and hid it in his backpack before stepping into the kitchen where all the other boys were hitting each other and laughing while JT was sitting down at the table of presents and dirty dishes and trash with a vanilla cake in front of him and an edible picture of Eminem frowning printed on it. J welcomed D by pulling him in with a one-arm hug, which was permissible because that's not totally gay, and then they sang Happy Birthday, the rot of the gray walls peeling, thunder roaring with the wind, a flicker of ceiling lights as moths suicidally flew into them, and then the birthday candles snuffed with smoke rising into the twilight of a cursed house and doomed twisted family, Happy Birthday, JT opens his presents, and roaches defecate among the waste of wrapping paper crumbled up on the floor.

Come October, when girls use a black sharpie to write 'Fuck Off' and draw a stick figure on a boy's converse shoe, when the cool air of decaying autumn sweeps through the pumpkin patch, recording Halloween specials of cartoons on VHS tapes, mother brews you homemade apple cider, and you'll never forget how sweet it tasted. Come October, when the Texas heat blisters every sore into a permanent scar, a chewed scab, the drifting miasma between a divine dream-world and traumatic night terrors. Come October, the cursed month where something was always bound to go wrong, like a failed suicide that led to vomiting out the chalk and being nailed to a hospital bed, to be thrown out onto the streets like a dog, big dummy's head emptying from a gunshot, a phone call signaling your lover will be dead in the coming months. To never let October come, when will it ever end, things will never be the same, the primordial fear, it's coming, again, there is death in the decaying driftwood and the first rain thickening the air, within your heart valves, your kidneys, those split wrists, that hole in his head. And so October comes relentlessly.

Most of the boys slept in the tent out in the backyard, while the rest were scattered upon furniture inside the house. D stared blankly at the canvas gray above him, concentrating on the wisp of the wind as it had begun to settle into a foreboding stillness. Homes weren't the only haunted places in Texas; the dead were lurking outside as well. After all, that's where Riley became a corpse, the blood puddle sinking from the gravel and into the grass. His best friend, J, slept like a baby with his elbows protruding into D's back, and the boy beside him couldn't rest. He was consumed by all the terrifying stories they made up all night and the horror movies they watched, with every sound outside of the tent magnified as something dangerous to him. D whispered to him to go inside if he was so scared, but the boy was too worried that if he left the tent, let alone move a muscle, something would capture him and take him out of his own body.

"Bloody Mary, Bloody Mary, Bloody Mary," D cursed slowly, attempting to frighten the boy more.

It wasn't long after he spoke the name that the shadow

of two people paced around their tent. Both boys observed cautiously, aware of each goosebump and chill that froze them to the core. No, it couldn't have been human, not with the kind of canine growls and huffs it had been making. The creature knelt and caressed the polyester tent in zig-zag lines. Something about how close it was made D want to vomit as if it were a zombified Riley that'd come back to cannibalize him. Several minutes later, it crawled away as if to vaporize with the wind, but only before shutting the rusted gate. Something else lifted D out of himself and directed him out of the tent. The sky was starless, the air was a void, and his eyes were a wasp nest. Once inside the house, he drifted through the rooms like a voyeur, gazing down on each of his friends as they slept, sensing the dread infecting their dreams. He crouched down carefully, crawled on the carpet, trimmed his nails against JT's door, and then headed into the kitchen, where one of the boys had been sitting as if paralyzed in a chair against the wall. The boy didn't seem confused about why D was on the floor. He, too, was being possessed by a creature spreading its death wings beyond the house.

"You're awake," D commented quietly. "Did you see it?"

The kid nodded. The tick of a clock was between them, which felt out of place because this should have been the dream world. He explained, "It was to the left of my face while I was playing Mario Party. I fell back, and then it was gone. I'm not going back in there. And I'm not going back to sleep."

As D stood up, he felt a hole opening up from his forehead. Drool was spilling from the ends of his mouth. He sat down beside his friend and assured him, "I'll stay awake for you. Go ahead and rest."

Instead, he fell asleep shortly after and woke up on the grimy kitchen tiles next to the roaches. The sunlight gleaming through the cracked windows felt other-worldly. Before stepping into the backyard, JT, J, and one of the other kids pulled him back as if it were a crime scene with a loved one being zipped up in a body bag. But he could still see out, past the tent, and at the strange spectacle beyond it. What appeared to be a human head was spiked through one of the met-al poles, dry blood caked all over it, a disfigured face seething toward him, both childish and ancient in ap-pearance, with a mop of wet black hair partially cover-ing the milky emerald eyes. But it was not human, nor was it some sort of Halloween decoration from Party City. Someone had made it themselves.

None of them knew who did it. JT's brother and his best friend were still in Denton. The neighbors were Christian zealots who protested Halloween, so it couldn't have been them. JT's stepfather called the police, but they wouldn't even take the fake severed head off the fence. The other boys hadn't thought of it, but D couldn't help but see the face as his own. He watched as JT's stepfather grunted, lifted the head off the pole, walked over to the black garbage can, and disposed of it.

Without looking at the others, D spoke to his friends, or maybe himself, "For some reason, I feel like I was decapitated in another life. Or maybe, I'll lose it in this life. Do you think someone was watching us all night, and that's why they put that there? Like... someone wants to cut off our heads?"

"That's sick, dude. What the heck." J laughed back at the idea. Some of the others shrugged, while the rest were too disturbed to know how to react or what to say. If anything, they could only try to forget it as best as possible and swear never to come back to JT's house. None of their parents wanted them to stay over anyway since they had already heard rumors of the broken family, the abuse and alcohol and drugs, a delinquent teenager, and the rapes.

Most of the kids didn't know the meaning behind the words JT used as he casually presented his thoughts, "It was probably one of the pedophiles that live near-by. Mom says there are tons all around our house. Maybe it wasn't such a good idea to camp out last night." He glanced at D for a second, then at the youngest boys. "We could've gotten raped."

Something about how he said the word raped made D's stomach churn. He was doing his best to forget it. To be another normal kid. A conforming little straight boy. With his eyes closed, he blacked out the image of someone cutting off his head with a kitchen knife, of Riley as a zombie pleasuring himself against their tent, and replaced it with a picture of himself naked on his bed. He imagined Riley looking down and ordering him around, "Show me your teeth. Smile wide. Good boy. Pretend you're at the dentist's office. Smile harder. Look at me and open your eyes."

X   X   X

Austin was a monolith, he was The Alamo, a tall blunt fortress, barely held together after the losing battle, his limestone skin easily overlooked by his baggy black jeans, a switchblade attached to his belt, the oversized Marilyn Manson t-shirt, he was the war that would never come to an end. Even as he sat slumped back in his computer chair in the dark, he seemed massive in height to D, a terrifying demon, casually murdering people with an assault rifle on a computer game. The two of them sat side by side and fell into the computer monitor's trance, the sound of soldiers crouched down and waiting for an enemy inside the basement of a power plant, the echo of a bullet, a corpse that would fall to the ground and bleed and vanish.

The bedroom lights were off, the windows draped with black curtains, and a wet towel was placed by the door so that the luster of the screen would illuminate them. They could barely hear their mothers outside and in the kitchen, let alone their own breaths. But their presence was still there, like a scar from a scab that would never heal.

"Fuck you, fucking die, piece of shit, fuckhead." Austin's words were thick with venom, not focused on the enemy somewhere across the planet but within the house itself. It was his slut of a mother, his know-it-all Catholic stepfather, his other faggot father, and his retarded, wannabe rapper brother. "Fucking dead, faggot. Dammit, fuck! Fuck you!"

As soon as he died, he shut off the monitor, which sunk the room into an abyss. D stood up once the lamp partially illuminated the room in a hue of lipstick-red.

"Wait. Before you go." There was a rare and profound grace in the teenager's voice. He took something out of his drawers and handed it to D. "Don't give it back to me. It's yours."

The boy held the object in both of his hands. It was heavier than he imagined it would be, and he couldn't think why he'd need it or how he'd even use it. Heavier than the Tanakh, he thought. He asked quietly, "What am I supposed to do with it? If my parents found this, they'd beat the heck out of me. My dad might even kill me."

"Yeah, that's what dads do. They beat you. Mom's just lie and manipulate you. I don't know, man. Just take it with you everywhere you go. You'll feel safer, stronger. Sometimes, I just like to hold them, look at them, and then my mind becomes static or like there's nothing there."

It felt magnetic in his tiny palms. He slid half of it under his shorts and underwear and hid the rest with his shirt. For some reason, it felt more like a curse than a gift. Unbeknown to Austin, he now possessed two of his knives.

D stepped backward until he tapped the edge of the bed and mouthed with a sense of harrowing fear, "Thank you."

Later that day, while he and his mother were at Target and buying pounds of Halloween candy, D raised his shirt in the middle of one of the aisles and finally looked at the leather sheath for the hunting knife given to him. 'I want to kill someone now,' he thought. 'But I don't know who I want to kill yet.'

They couldn't find him the costume he was looking for at Target or Walmart, but they did restock more orange lights for the bushes in the front yard. As much as he pleaded to his parents, even after showing them the links on eBay and other websites so that he could buy the Danny Phantom costume he had dreamed of wearing for the past few months, they wouldn't do it for him. However, after they had driven to Frisco, D's mother got him a Robin Hood costume and promised to paint his face like a fox on Halloween night and Friday for Kids Night Out.

During the week at school and daycare, D brought the knife with him in his backpack. Since he was always the first student dropped off in the morning, he'd spend his time in the bathroom or lost in hallways gazing at his knife instead of reading articles about nebulas and comets on Wikipedia. He'd check his backpack repeatedly to ensure the weapon was still there whenever he had the chance. Austin was right. It gave him a sense of security and power over everyone else. He liked the danger of it, too. A part of him wanted to be caught, especially by the teacher who gyrated him once and had him thrown into a closet. In the past, he always feared that some mass murderer would randomly break in and shoot him and all of his classmates, but now he wanted it to happen more than ever. He wanted to see his friends blown to pieces, especially his teachers, and whether he could or not, he wanted to use his knife to kill the intruder.

And yet, he could still hear the innocent repetitive songs from Blue's Clues, the fluffy dog barking at the back of his head, and the talking paprika spice. Andromeda was still visible in ultraviolet behind his eyes at night. There were notebooks of codes that he and

J were still putting together for future websites and flash games. A VHS tape of The Goonies that he had watched a thousand times would still be played once more while he cuddled beside his mother as if to become nonexistent in her presence and into the steaming astral waters where The Goonies pirate ship was once hidden. Life was nothing more than the tape of a movie slowly being scratched and ruined until it was unreadable, swarming in static and white noise, with a million ghosts lost and drowning in every blinking epileptic spec.

X   X   X

"You know that you're a fuckin' faggot, right?"

D wasn't looking at Austin when he spoke to him. The line of kids buying candy and soda vanished as they squirmed into the vibrant dance room and the loud thundering gymnasium. Then there were the sounds of screaming children, basketballs slamming into bone-white brick walls, cheesy R&B, everyone singing along, the shrill haunted breeze of the back-door gusting behind the two boys, and a boombox playing Eiffel 65's 'Blue' on Disney's radio channel for the third time in an hour.

"If you were straight, you would have immediately reacted and said something like, fuck you, I'm not a faggot, you're a faggot, faggot fuck. But you didn't. You don't even know you're gay yet, but it's obvious. You try to hide it. Walk like you're straight, force your vocal cords down, you try not to look at other guys, but I see it. I know it. You're so quiet and scared of me all of a sudden because you know I'm right. Go ahead and say it. Say that you're a fucking faggot."

D looked down at his half-empty cup of root beer, feeling dizzy like spinning teacups; sometimes, he had fourteen fingers, and other times he had seven. His lips perched and rumbled as if he were about to break into an incredible sob. The ten-year-old asked confusedly, "I thought we were cool, now. We're not friends?"

Somewhere on the dance floor, JT was freestyling in front of other white kids and hitting on black girls without realizing half of the pick-up lines he used were racist. The Whisper Song by The Ying Yang Twins would play with half of the words censored, and kids would sing every dirty lyric out loud. Jasmine and Sterling would be sitting near the DJ and pressed against the windows, staring at the brewing storm that never seemed as if it would come, while they wondered if D had abandoned them again.

"So what's up with the costume, anyway, faggot? You're Robin Hood, huh? Like the cartoon? Do you like to fuck animals, too?"

The boy gripped the table, dug his nails into tar, carved holes previously dug out from pencils and pens, sickened with rage, hatred for the world, and disgust for himself. His memories were plagued with a blaring trombone, a cacophonous clarinet, violins screeching, and a mournful symphony triumphant over mindless techno coming from next door. He thought of all the times he masturbated to the Robin Hood cartoon movie, or how much he wanted to be Simba from The Lion King and raped by the villainous Scar, or how he used to breakdance in an empty garage pretending to be Beyonce and Ciara and imagine himself as charismatic and beautiful as Usher in the Confessions, Pt. II music video.

"What you faggots do. It's fucking disgusting. What my dad did to us, that rich faggot piece of shit can get away with anything now. And it doesn't matter what was done to you. Every single faggot is a pedophile and a rapist. You're not one yet, but you will be someday. And so I fucking hate all of you. Sick. Fucking disgusting. It makes me want to fucking vomit all over and kill you all. The worst is that you're a faggot Jew. We need another Holocaust."

With his eyes forming Sirius stars that could turn black holes into white diamonds, D echoed back to him, "You know you're a faggot, right?" There was silence, so he wasn't sure Austin noticed or was affected by what he said, so he repeated it and laughed at himself, "You know you're a faggot, too, right?"

The silence lingered as the queer autumn nightmare seeped into their misty skulls. Dead leaves were glowing lemon yellow, lavender, and vermillion at their feet. Death marked them both while they weren't looking.

Austin finished his paper cup, crushed it with one hand, and quietly remarked, "I'm confused."

When D stood up, it was as if he was lifted out of his body by something else, and suddenly, everything became an illusory fanfare. All Austin could do was glare at his back in shock as he walked away while other children were running to D's table to buy sodas and candy. The music was blasting louder and faster than before, out with the sleazy R&B and in with the dance remixes of hardcore rap hits. Even the kids outside the dance room were rocking faster, their bodies as prisoners to the beat, a contagious mania plaguing the lone star community center. And The Kids Night Out dance floor went ballistic to Freek-A-Leek, fucking radiant shards of crystalized light splintering from out their eyes mouths chests cascading and glowing and opening gateways to parallel existences into the ceiling far from out of their reach, the false heaven, tongue kiss in the limbo, this place was pure hell. Texas can only be a purgatory downward spiral into the devil's guts for the children destined to die within it.

"You okay, D?"

Jasmine and Sterling had chrome angel wings growing out of their shoulders that sprinkled fairy dust over the river of sweat on the ground. They were the only ones that weren't moving to the left, right, backing it up, stopping, wiggling it. What D couldn't see were his own silver wings, a hlue like dust and mold and dirty snow, fluttering painfully behind him, attempting to fly, to take him away from this world of rape and lies, but he was more like a bird crashing into a window, collapsing and frozen in shock moments before death.

Fists were shot into the air, hips and elbows blossomed tentacles, the kids bounced to chopped synths, frigid Vocaloid voices, swam into each other, became sentient beings, only to separate once again, a festering and anxious screaming of unified flesh was exploding. They shouted lyrics as if to cut their own throats. They gave up the freedom of their souls to the music and hoped it would free them from the foes of coming adulthood. They could escape the post 9/11 with-

-in a song. Rewind Katrina. Cross out the oil wars. Dale Earnhardt brought back to life. D had much to forget and displace as well. Regardless of whether he liked the music, his angel wings fluttered into the mess of kids he didn't know, and he abandoned his true friends to dance mindlessly with strangers. They took him in as one of them, followed his movements, taught them their own, howled, and clapped at his ability to absorb the rhythm. The exploding carcass- es of half angels half aliens poisoned by Raytheon war machines radiated the heat death rage and ecstatic orgasm inside them as they climbed the walls to the epileptic uplifting trance music. Light spilled out, they underwent cybernetic transformation, and translucent diamonds obliterated their bodies until their souls became their own detonator. The walls were melting neon, hyper cyber metal wolf teeth, and the floor be- came a fog-filled snake pit. They intended to leave the dance floor swamped with a stew of guts and ground bone dust filtering from out of the windows and to wreak havoc in the humid air. They'd suicide-pill the planet. All skyscrapers and hidden lake-side man- sions would collapse into gaping wounds inside of the earth. A dance to dismantle every colonial mon- ument. High-rise freeways would cave into the pave- ment. And the doomed children would dance on. The rave crept away from D's auditory visions, and echoes of The Cure began consuming him, an instrumental ballad, a favorite of Riley's, like a bullet through the head. Somewhere behind the DJ, Bloody Mary was laughing hysterically at him.

Once D finally made it back to Jasmine, he clasped her hands in his own, and felt the electricity from his skin to sweat merge with her. His mouth hung open as his tongue felt swollen and picked at his gums while millions of dots spread across his vision. D's shoulders swept as he sputtered, "You can't save me from what has, is, and will happen to me, you, or all of us, but you could at least dance with me. I'll dance for the life I want to live, and if I can't have it, G-d please lift me to heaven."

Sterling was being swathed and tossed around by a sea of limbs conglomerating into one sentient being. The more he pushed through, the further he felt from them. He could see D guiding Jasmine into his dance.

The raven-haired boy faced his palm to the ground and continued, "Can't you feel that -- the earth rattling? I can feel whatever's happening to me within the core. We have to dance, forget every notion of our lives, and pretend that we'll be kids like this forever. I don't fucking care about anything anymore. It's all fucked up."

As D collapsed to the ground, Jasmine's body rose to the ceiling, stretched across it all, glowing lilac, and a song emerged from her that blanketed all muzak out. It was a harmonious drone, with female vocals fading in and out. He shook his head, knowing that half of what he saw couldn't be real, and crawled on elbows and knees out of the dance room as drool pooled out from his mouth.

Sterling thought about following D to the bathroom when he saw his friend rush into it, shaking and possessed, but Jasmine stopped him. What kind of friend was he, anyway? To turn them down so that D could stay at JT's another night, that white kid that says the 'N-word and wants to be a rapper, along with the psycho criminal older brother? Let him realize later on what kind of trouble he's in.

The restroom seemed like its own pocket universe stranded in a starless void. It was like any other restroom of his life. After pulling on his stomach and dry heaving into a urinal, he backed into a cracked sink and stared into an open stall. 'You should be with me in here,' He thought. 'Friendship bracelets…' A spark of malevolent hate overtook him, and he kicked at the stall's door, let it ricochet from the wall, and kicked it repeatedly until the sound reminded him of a gunshot and scared him.

Ectoplasm emerged from the drain next to the toilet. It swirled upward, expanded, and revealed itself as the blood bath Riley left behind but could never be bleached clean. After staining and poisoning everything, it had come to consume him finally. The next time D opened his eyes, he was inside Riley's mouth, standing behind his uvula, gazing into pink gummy flesh sticky with a velvet paste and remnants of gunpowder. A few back teeth were lodged into gums, shattered, enormous chunks. His angel wings crept back into his skin as he traversed away from the throat and through a ridged hole through the nostrils and top part of the skull. With a kick of his Converse shoes, he leaped from one bridge to the next and passed through another hallway until he reached a theater room. The screen was the right eye. The seats were made of muscle and tendons, and each had a remote on the armrests constructed from shards of the slimy ejected iris. At first, D was terrified of the room but felt that it was where he was meant to come to terms with everything, his past lives, birth, present, death, and subsequent lives and deaths as well.

On the first channels were a stream of films related to the Holocaust, Nuit et brouillard, Shoah by Lanzmann, Come and See, Europa Europa, Au revoir les enfants. After passing the classic film selections, he came upon moments of his future life. The boy he had once stood across from in the daycare bathroom was older and knocked all the schoolbooks out of his hands. Girls giggled as the boy called D a faggot and calmly collapsed into his desk in a stoned-out haze. This would be his future, a mop of messy black hair and razor lines across his wrists with the aftertaste of psych meds burning a hole in his stomach and clogging his brain. And there he was again, older, pulled down from a noose by his mother and brought back to life in a hospital, raped again, abused again, and again, and again, homeless, finding love, and then exiting a hospital room after saying goodbye to his dead lover. Wherever there was hope, there would also be more trauma and death. This would be the life he could inherit and then some. He thought about skipping past the other channel, being that it was about the corpse and/or spirit that he was inside of, but he went back to it, not out of curiosity, but to torture himself. Through Riley's eyes, he saw predatory hands in front of him that were now his, which reached under bedsheets to grope through a pair of briefs while a boy slept. Riley's face was buried into his hair, breathing heavily like boulders from mountains of snow, his erection throbbing against a well-used opening. When the boy woke up, he cupped one hand over his mouth, and the other, once digging at a piss hole, was ready to strangle him to death. This was Riley as a kid. He was not raped as a child. Yes, the parents fought, and sometimes his father hit him and raped his mother, but what he was doing was something he enjoyed from as early as he could remember.

Others fed feral cats while he shot them and drove over their dead bodies with his dad's truck. On the next channel was a CCTV broadcast of the backyard where Riley's body remained unanimated, along with the flashes of Halloween lights from police cars in the background behind the recently painted fence.

After he shut off the screen with the remote, the theater descended into an abyss. D blinked with Riley's eyes, exited the theater of the dead mind, and returned to the restroom universe. His evanescent angel wings shook away what he had seen; dashes of white crystals shattered to the tiles. The toilet stall was spattered with blood and brain matter; it was as if someone had popped a balloon filled with red dye. Fear was inaccessible within this vacuum of intimate nightmares, and what the boy saw only made him feel more sluggish and depersonalized. His hands traced along the white caulking between bricks until he exited the bathroom and entered the main game room, which had been empty of kids, almost silent except for the hum of electric static and the brisk howl of wind against nature and glass. He remembered the intestines of the mall where he had been molested for the first time by a stranger, which felt similar to this. But in that instance, the man had mysteriously transferred him from a bathroom to hidden hallways that could only be accessed with a key card or through the storage rooms of stores and kitchens. Had everyone gone home and forgotten that he existed?

In front of the foosball, air hockey, and pool tables were towering glass windows being scraped by bur oak trees' fingernails. D moved closer to admire how minuscule he felt in their presence. This loneliness inspired by the woods outside brought him contempt toward the idea of his coming death. He remembered the graveyard near his grandmother's house, which stretched out for miles along undulating hills, trees as lush and colossal as any other he'd seen, a place that brought him peace, where hundreds of corpses rested in filthy worm and dirt-infested coffins. A boy had been killed near there, somewhere between that graveyard and her house. They found his skeleton hidden in a deep crevice of dying earth. He'd been raped and killed, and once he was buried properly, his tombstone was stolen, never to be found. How could D ever forget about that? When he first heard about it, he was obsessed and researched it as much as possible but couldn't find anything online. Did his face look just like D's? Would that have been him at some point if Riley hadn't taken his own life? 'That kid is me,' he'd prophesize. 'I'm just not him yet. No -- I'm already dead. I've never been alive, have I? And I just keep dying.'

Riley's bisected and rotten zombified corpse was hanging from a cross between two glass windows, far out of D's reach. He was unrecognizable now. Stitches pulled apart Riley's zombie's eyelids. The figure vanished like a hallucination, and D angered himself by thinking about how he wanted to befriend Riley again and forget their past few days together had ever happened. But it was only a hallucination. The reality is that the rapist was dead, a fitting end to a worthless, demented life.

"Hello?" D spoke quietly, allowing his prepubescent voice to echo through every empty room. "JT? Sterling? J?" It was like he was in a horror film, where a character is lost after splitting up and spouting random names until the killer is nearby. Everyone had gone home. He didn't exist in this world anymore. The boy questioned himself, 'I'm alone, but I've always been alone, haven't I?' He pressed his face against the glass of a door, closed his eyes, and remembered his past Octobers. There were pumpkin and ghost-shaped noodles in the Mac N' Cheese that he made for himself and green Frankenstein faces on sugar cookies and the scent of roasted seeds, and the VHS tape wrapped around his little fingers and bowls of candy and waiting for someone to come home and the holiday candles his mother was selling around the neighborhood and when he slit open his thumb making Spaghetti-O's, but nobody was home, and when Riley was in a different room filled with scorpions while D watched reruns of The Simpson's Treehouse of Horror's episodes on DVD and when he first watched the cartoon version of The Hobbit at his grandmother's house while she baked cookies for troops in Iraq, the sound of his father's pacemaker ticking as he rested on his chest, mother nowhere to be found, she was selling purses and lingerie and sobbing in the closet, and Robin Hood on repeat in his dreams when the nightmares weren't all-consuming. The facepaint was beginning to smudge and flicker off his forehead and cheeks. Soon, his mask would slip off, and he would only be a boy, again, the faggot child.

As if it were a misplaced timelapse within a dream, he found himself wandering outside the community center, drawn closer to the woods, and following the eternal rhythm of the hidden creek. He knelt down and dug one hand into the wet grass to feel the dirt. The crisp smell of organic decay pierced his chest. Riley was in there. Everyone. As one. In another life, he was one of his distant cousins, he was his mother and father, he was himself, but even more tortured, and he was also Riley, and even the others. They were all alive and dead within him.

His head slammed into the grass and blood trickled down his neck while a thundering boom consumed his entire nervous system. When he crawled onto his back, he saw two teenagers above him, one with a bat and the other with a rope. Both boys worked at the community center, so it made sense that they would be the last ones there. D sat up on his elbows, confused and horrified. He knew at this point that he had been drugged earlier on, and this must have been their plan all along.

Austin vehemently hounded him, "Say it. Say that you're a faggot right now. Take his stupid fucking skullcap off already. We'll fucking kill you if you don't admit it, kike."

The yarmulke came off and was thrown down the slope leading to the creek. Sam went down to grab him by the legs, and the little fox squirmed out of his hands, which made Austin want to take another swing, but the two were all over each other now. Angel wings were blooming again. Both teens were fighting to gain control of the resistant boy, and as rope fell from Sam's hands, D lifted his shirt, took out the knife that had been gifted to him, and inserted it into a welcoming throat. The blade exited out like butter, it felt like magic to kill him, and then it was Sam on the grass with blood spraying out of his throat.

"Fucking faggot! Fucking kike!" Austin cried out as he reached for the bat, but the boy was already on top of him. Even though he was heavier than D, the fear had locked him into fight or flight. His vision went crimson and blurry, the baseball bat had rolled too far away, and suddenly, he felt a jab in his guts. As Austin's body rattled with electricity, he used his other hand to reach behind his back and regained control when he sideswiped the kid with a gun. The pain in Austin's side, like a sewing needle through a finger, meant nothing to him now, and in a matter of seconds, he was above the faggot child, and managed to pull the trigger before it could react again.

D collapsed beside the other dead boy, but there wasn't nearly as much blood over his face as there was pooling out of Sam's neck. Instead, it leaked silently from the back of his head and into the dirt, blood into roots that would find Riley, his other selves, until it would reach the tree that a piece of him was buried under, and the tree would rot and split apart into a million parts.

When Austin looked away from D, he saw a spirit hovering close to him. Worms and maggots infested the nebulous face. It pointed at him and reminded the teenager of his mortal wound; he hadn't realized that when D went to stab him, the blade went halfway through his stomach. His clothes were caked with blood. Even though it would stop oozing from the outside, the inside would soon hemorrhage. It would only be a matter of time before he became a ghost and trapped on the dying planet. The spirit came closer, reminding him that he had been born only as a vessel of humanity's evil, and even though he was now weak, the devil would take care of and guide him. This is how it had always been, Cain and Abel, him versus the father who raped him and JT, or in the case of Riley and D, and so on.

The spirit entered his body, and Austin was left with only fragments of himself. It helped him tie D and his friend's arms and legs, roll them down the hill and into a lake, reload the gun, and drive him back home. The world was beginning to blur, and it would remain like that forever.

Several spirits greeted him when he opened the front door to his house, Bloody Mary, the woman who had previously lived there, and the entity inside and outside his own body. They guided him around the decorated house, dimly lit with purple lights inside of plastic spiders. His reflection beamed back at him through the swaying kitchen window, pale and pasty, the smeared eyeliner, chunks of gel caked into his dyed jet-black hair. D had been right about him all along. He believed that killing him would have liberated him from his self-hate. Instead, he would soon die, and the only thing left was the sobbing self-pity he collapsed into near the sink and the consummation of the dead comforting him.

"Hey. JT. Wake up." The bald kid opened his eyes. His brother was sitting on his chest with the gun to his chin. "Die, faggot." He pulled the trigger. This was the only thing that made sense to him. The spirit commanded, 'Erase your family. Erase yourself. I'll make you pure.' JT's jaw was split in two, blood-spattered all across the bed, onto Austin's legs, spraying and gushing in geysers. He pulled the trigger again. This time, he aimed at the forehead. The back of the skull exploded, the scent of gunpowder was noxious, and he looked less like the brother he loved and wanted to protect and more like some mummy unwrapped from its tomb. He thought, 'Humans aren't meant to look like this.' Then he fell into the mangled lobes, the nos-

-trils, of the face that looked more like an efflorescent rose. 'Fuck… I'm so sorry, JT. I'm so fucking sorry.'

The gunshots woke up his parents, and Austin's step-father was hastening to load his shotgun. The man blasted the door apart as soon as it creaked open, and another gunshot cracked within the room. Austin's mother screamed. At first, she caved herself into the bedsheets, but as her son approached her, she wriggled her thin, anorexic, and mutilated limbs to the corpse she loved, kissed its face, and attempted to wake her lover by caressing his chin and chest. The dead man's legs were still dancing to the shock, and it throttled a bit more when Austin shot into it a few more times. She screamed as if to tear herself from the world, but it wasn't necessary. "Shut the fuck up," he yelled back at his demented mother. But she couldn't stop herself from screaming. Standing above the limp whore, he squeezed the trigger again. It exhilarated him more than any of the other killings. She had fucked him into this existence with a man who would rape him and his younger brother. He always found it pathetic that she'd slash her wrists and burn her hands with cigarette butts in shame. Wouldn't it make more sense to stop toying around and kill herself?

Austin didn't need to be reminded by the spirit of what he had to do next. It didn't matter if it were by his own hands either because he knew he would soon bleed to death next to his mother's corpse. It didn't feel right to die beside them. They weren't a family; they were an amalgamation of unfixable mistakes at-tempting to mask themselves behind a veil of normal-cy when everyone knew it was a lie. Riley reassured him, 'It's better like this. All of you can be angels now.

This is the only path to purity for the cursed. People think you can live in hope, that time will heal, and new wings will liberate you from the evil and trauma inflicted on you, but that's an unrealistic narrative built out of fear. X'd out. You're forever fucked. And the only way out is to die quickly before that belief imprisons you. Hope is the most destructive force of all. Now kill yourself.'

The second that Austin's feet left his mother's bedroom carpet and to the wooden floorboards of the hallway, he put the gun to the back of his head and did as the spirit told him. Dead without angel wings sprouting from his back, still a faggot, and his father, who lived thirty-five miles away in Frisco, was having an expensive dinner at Longhorn Steakhouse with his new family.

X   X   X

When they found D's corpse, it hadn't even bloated, and the boy's hair shrouded the hole inside of his head, which gave the illusion to the paramedics and officers that he could somehow, in some mystic way, be alive. There was a strange grace attached to his still form. When they brought him to the grass, his arms were crossed over his chest, the rope that had once been tied to his legs had come unbound, and he wore only a pair of white briefs while the rest of him had still been cherubic. It's as if all that had been done to him had been washed away in the lake. What was left was the most supreme form of innocence that had graced their eyes. Before the body bag was zipped up, a paramedic clipped his yarmulke back onto his head. This would not be the end of his mummification, but it was enough to allow him to drift off peacefully and into heaven.

Others would have to suffer from grief on a collapsing planet while he rejoined the thread of light that connected him to all of his previous and future lives. There would be a mother unable to hold her daughter for months because squeezing her son's Star Wars sith blanket was the only thing that brought her comfort when she cried. A year before he died, he tried to kill himself with her medication. At that point, all of her fears were confirmed, and she knew she would eventually have to bury him before her own death.

She continued to work without ever holding onto any fragment of hope. Two weeks off was all she could get; capitalism and corporations didn't pay her any sympathy as she continued to sell purses and lingerie at the mall. In the grocery store, in traffic, in the public bathroom, she would suddenly burst into a frantic rage and sob, beat her face with her fists, grit her teeth, and scream at the ground. Nothing would help, nothing would ever bring him back, and she still had to be a mother to a new child.

Her husband had to be the lifeline, even if his health continually declined. He hid it better than her, but sometimes he took it out on the furniture or the car wheel in the parking garage of the community college.

They'd make more money and get a bigger house, yet the ghosts would haunt that home as well.

'What hope could be left, and was there any in the first place,' the mother often wondered. 'Maybe it's better this way. No matter what, he was going to suffer forever. There's no way he would've ever gotten better with what happened to him.' And then the realization that she repeated to herself every waking moment of the day, 'It will never get better for any of us.'

X   X   X

J would remember it all. When his mother would say goodnight before heading downstairs, he'd notice the nightlight on his dresser and smirk, thinking of how D would tease him for being scared of the dark. He thought of when he saw D cry when he was smacked in the face with a soccer ball or how D begged his parents not to let him play baseball anymore after he was hit in the leg. What it had been like when they first saw each other naked and how gay he felt thinking about the differences in their genitals. There was a folder of audio recordings in his My Documents folder, where they made chipmunk remixes of pop songs and recordings of D pretending to be a radio host.

"Welcome to the funny bunny radio show," D would announce in his high-pitched, queer faggot voice. "And today's guest is… BEYONCE! Woohoooooooo ~ Baby boy, ah dah dah dah, fulfill my fantasy. Alright, everybody, it's joke time! Who wants to hear a funny joke? Oh, me, me!" J felt terrible laughing at how stupid and gay the two of them used to act.

In an attempt to forget, he deleted the audio files. He deleted the stop-motion movies they made with Legos and his dead gerbil. And he deleted the videos they made where they pretended to kill each other multiple times with toy weapons. He remembered telling D that the footage they recorded at night to capture evidence of ghosts had been deleted, but that was a lie. It would take him many more years before he would finally stumble upon the hidden file and watch it again.

When D's parents gave him his friend's computer, he decided to let it collect dust in his closet until he felt it was also ready to be destroyed. What was on it would have only distorted the image everyone had of D, the tortured gracious Jewish boy murdered and rotting in the ground and dressed in his best forest green clothes and a tallit that embraced him like a blanket. That's the image he needed to preserve as a memory of his friend, not the gay porn he found the one time he plugged it in.

Nor did he want to continue imagining what he saw in that hidden video of the spirit, which seemed to have more interest in his friend than him, and how D woke up in a panic, went back to bed, and never told him about it. The nightmares must have been common. What he went through, he couldn't even imagine. As he grew older, everything made more sense; he understood why D had to move in with him for that short time, why his friend often talked of wanting to die, and how sexual he was. He was happy that D didn't come back to haunt him, which assured him that D was in a better place and that J was loved and would always be protected by him.

X   X   X

When D's mother saw her son's tombstone for the first time, the first thing she focused on was the Magen David - not his name and not the day he was born or his death day; those are things she already remembered vividly and could torture herself over some other time. She thought about whether or not it was appropriate, if D really believed in a higher power or not, that maybe she was too outspoken about her denouncement of organized religion, and what kind of messages she signaled to him about being a Jew. She planned to stop taking him to services after his Bar Mitzvah at thirteen because it was only an act for her parents. Then she remembered a conversation she had with D at the sculpture garden in Fort Worth, when she explained to him that even though she was an atheist, she would still be considered a Jew forever because it was culture and ethnicity, whereas D's father, who'd been raised Christian and was now an atheist, was just an atheist. She told him Christians didn't have to sacrifice anything or worry about how their identity could hold them hostage in America. They can convert by effortlessly saying, "I believe in Jesus," and that's all it would take. Being a Jew is different. It's like this, she explains. You're supposed to wear that yarmulke, and in a just world, you could every day, but you can't because people will hate you and tease you for it, and even when you don't wear it, people will somehow still know, and they'll hate and tease you for it, too. A Christian doesn't have to wear a cross. They don't have to eat a certain way their entire life or fast multiple times a year. The reason she first wanted to stop raising him as a Jew after his Bar Mitzvah was due to him being given an IDF shirt at his synagogue, proudly wearing it once a week, and believing in what other kids had told him about Israel, how they were doing the right thing to Palestine. But now, her palm was against the Star, which felt like a distant white dwarf in a galaxy of wrecked planets. What if this idea of a G-d could have saved him, and maybe he'd live to see a Bar Mitzvah, and instead of growing disinterested in faith and his ancestral history, it would be the star to heal him of all the fucked up shit that happened to him. Christians believed that everything was predestined and happened for a reason, and from what she learned, or at least what she was told by D, who paid more attention and had more interest in Judaism than her, Jews didn't believe in destiny; Jews believed G-d gave humans free will. The issue, a Hebrew teacher told D, is that humans have abused their free will in the hope of achieving G-d-like power, leading to obscene horrors like the crusades and the Holocaust. More personally, D being raped by a pedophile that could have easily admired but never touched him or just fucked off. Which was worse, she thought to herself while kneeling on the dried grass by his arched tombstone, a G-d that made it your destiny to be raped and killed, or a G-d that let it happen because he decided he had already done enough by giving birth to such a terrifying species?

When D's father saw his son's tombstone for the first time, the first thing he focused on was his name. It wasn't D on the gravestone. It was the name he had chosen, along with the Hebrew name that they decided on as well. D's real name was T. T was named after his father's childhood best friend, who died in a car crash a few years before his birth. It was common to name a newborn Jew after a dead family member or a loved one, so T seemed fitting, even if it was a Christian name. He thought about how that was his idea, and even though he didn't believe in a higher power, if G-d did exist, maybe the T that was dead longer than his son would feel honored, like his name would become a beautiful legend, and it would be infinite. When someone dies, you want them to live forever, and grief will make you do whatever it wants you to do to preserve that notion. So he'd raise T to be all the things he loved, football and the Dallas Cowboys and baseball and the Texas Rangers and science fiction shows and Star Wars because that was him, and every time he said his son's name, he was also saying his own name, and his best friend's name. Now both of them were dead. He imagined the two T's finally meeting and if they would be friends in heaven forever or if his son would talk to him for a few minutes but grow bored, thinking, 'Why can't I just be back on earth, hanging out with J, instead?' When D first found out why he was named T, he adapted a fear of cars and believed he, too, would die in a car crash. G-d didn't write that, but his father must have, somehow, by giving him that stupid, embarrassing name. And since he was a boy that hated cars, that must have made him even more of a faggot child in his father's eyes. The kids that did like D called him that because he looked like a boy in a horror movie, and that felt fitting to him, so he went with it forever, and then everyone called him D instead of his birth name. The tombstone was half of a lie. He wanted to knock it over, crush half of it into chunks of granite, and leave only the Magen and the day of his birth. That would be enough for them to remember.

G-d was everywhere and in everything and let D's mother live through years of abuse and neglect and attempted suicide, and cursed D's father with a heart condition from the early age of six that would require open-heart surgeries every decade for the rest of his life and then G-d allowed them to make a child, and then G-d watched closely as the child was molested and then the child was raped and almost killed and raped more and then he was killed. What the Hebrew teacher told D is that G-d cries when bad stuff happens to innocent people, he wants to do something, but he can't, which means that G-d was also in mourning with his parents. And it wasn't like D was in a better place. In all realities, he would suffer, and in all forms of himself, he was bound to be hurt.

What they weren't thinking about was the thing D always thought about when he walked with his grandmother during summertime in Iowa at the nearby graveyards. 'Isn't it strange that people are always standing over your dead body and praying at a stone or slab in the ground and not directly at where you're buried? It's like how people stare at the sky as if G-d is there and not all over.' He hoped nobody would stand on his grave and instead pray or speak directly at his rotting corpse, but that would never happen. And he hoped that the name he preferred to go by would be on his grave, but that would also never happen.

X   X   X

D feels the bullet opening a wormhole through his skull and thinks about Riley's death. He wanted it to be this way, so he's not terrified by it. In his twisted mind of Stockholm's, he was already convinced Riley should have been alive, not himself. Now, this shit story would be over, and he wouldn't have to experience any other tragedies life would offer him before an even more pointless death. This is better because you receive sympathy, whereas if his suicide attempt had worked last year, he would have been hated for it and eventually erased from everyone's memory.

The wound reconstructs into a similar space he occupies until his body is found. Black water. A black hole. Which opens its mouth, spiraling, sucking, consuming, and resuscitating everything that passes through it. When D exits one side and enters the other part of his skull, that's when his soul leaves his body, when his alabaster angel wings carry him off and into the theater of his own mind of decomposing mush. All but two flickering lights are off, the concessions stand is closed, and there's only one hallway leading to three different showings, all of which are interpretations of the same story. The door to the center is blocked off by plywood nailed to the bottom and top edges. Both that film and the one to the right were shot the same day he was born, which means his future life, the one where none of this happened, must be over there. He doesn't even consider that showing because he knows that film exhausts its maximal narrative in ways he never wants to imagine. However, the door to the left was shot four years after his mother was born. It's his film, even though he's never seen it before.

D rushes to his seat when he enters the theater because the movie has already started, meaning he's already missed so many vital scenes. It's a monochrome flashback, his father as a boy much younger than himself but looking exactly like him, and there's an IV hooked to his arm, which is not only filled with plasma but minuscule silver star stickers. It cuts to a scene of D's mother at the age of eight. A tornado is shredding apart a cornfield, and his mother and grandmother are speeding down the highway to get back to their house. In seconds, storm clouds like iron and steel have draped the skies, and the hail and rain are as heavy as the splinters of everything aggressively scattering down on them. They rescue their puppies and dogs and continue driving from one rural town with a population of a few hundred to the next, never looking back on that house that exists only like a scab from then on.

In the next scene, the protagonist gazes at the galaxy, back when light pollution wasn't a global issue. For a moment, he's a kid resting on a bale of hay on Earth, eternally adrift in the cosmos of wonder, where everything is a gorgeous question mark that doesn't need an answer. G-d made this, yet nobody seems to admire it except him. Maybe, one day in the near future, when spaceships like the Millennium Falcon exist, he could finally make it to Saturn and live there forever. He blows into a bass clarinet, sings to the universe, and the title screen blankets the stars.

D is no longer in the theater because he's in the ether waiting to become an accident and is also starring in the film. He has to see his way through the rest of the movie if he wants to make sense of himself. It's also another Jewish film; he hopes it won't be entirely about the shoah. Still, he expects that the ending will be sentimental and bittersweet but also end up on a twisted note, just like the other versions did.

AN

IOWA

TAIL

You were born within a lake, blessed by sapphire, and placed beside your sobbing mother upon a newly knitted quilt. Her eyes and her breasts and her voice weren't the first things that you had recognized from outside of the womb; it was the meadows that surrounded you, the oak trees stirring into each other, the sound of the river creek that followed you out of birth and into the world, the somber sky gyrating downward a hundred and fifty miles away, the acres of untainted soybeans, the sound of wind whistling like a bass clarinet. Yes, it was truly a miracle, in the days when most children seemed to be born dead with an umbilical cord around their neck, or conceived by evil means, whereas you were a thought-out plan as a gift to your brother and sister and cousins.

The quilt was given to your mother from a family at the end of town. They had helped your family establish their farmland back in 1939 when your grandparents settled into the bare alien lands. Images of stuffed teddy bears and dancing lambs were stitched into the fabric with dozens of vermillion hearts. Once you realized what animals they were, it confused you to know that the brown bear families would replicate strange cartoon versions of themselves over the blanket. Foxes would never do such a thing. Nor would there be ceramic angel children on mantels or crosses over the beds. There would be glass eyes nailed to the kitchen wall, a painting of the ten commandments, a curved mezuzah by a creaking screen door, plates and cups and knives with Hebrew on them, but not a single symbol of an animal within the family of foxes.

Once you were older, your mother told you several times that you were the perfect baby; you never cried or screamed or seemed to grow hungry, although, at one point, you did have an ear infection for several months that almost killed you. Your brother and sister were the opposite. Then it was your mother that became the cumbersome infant. With your brother dead from a car crash and your older sister either cursed by a dybbuk or suddenly Schizophrenic after being raped and beaten and left for dead on the side of the gravel road four miles from home, how else could a mother ever cope again?

The moment the sun peaked out from the woods that hid the river and until infinite stars would blanket the world, you, your living brother and father, would harvest soybeans and detassel corn, primarily by hand, along with cutting and baling hay. There was never a reward of thank you or good job when the work was done and certainly not any money, but if one thing was done wrong, your father made sure you'd remember the mistake for the rest of your life. When work was slow, you'd go to other farms around town, where money could be made. After the harvesting season was complete, you'd spend as much time living in your relative's houses. They would pretend to take you in as their son, an innocent, a serene and elegant soul that could do no wrong.

Every member of the family knew how to sing and play several instruments. You used to dance with your clarinet and giggle with glee as you improvised tunes on an accordion while your brother and sister sang in unison, but now everyone had been staring through their vision reflected on a TV screen or trapped to a damp mattress inside of their nebulous bedroom. Still, the music came to you. Maybe you were trying to hold onto it as much as possible as if it were the only thing to prevent you from losing faith in G-d.

Music was the kindness of caring for your cousin with Down syndrome, it was the gift that brought everyone together, it was the instrument that brought grace instead of an act to break one's chastity, it was the ether and the void, the sound of the river when you were born, and it would someday be the sound of your ascension to heaven. But one day, you'd see that music wasn't everything, and some things cannot be healed by art, even the purest and strongest forms of love. There would always be a hell cascaded over your earth, and it would promise that every soul connected to yours would be bound for the most profound forms of suffering and the ugliest deaths.

Somehow, she survived. None of her bones snapped or ripped through her flesh. A few weeks later, after she left the psychiatric hospital and spent several weeks walking with crutches, she wanted to do it all over again.

Of all people to live in the world, she would learn how to suffer more than anyone else. She would carry the pain and trauma of past generations on her shoulders, learn to live with her own, and someday, pass it down to someone else. Two thousand years of genocide and ethnic cleansing would be etched into her DNA and follow her wherever she went, whether she realized it or not. Even if she were to assimilate and someday confuse Hebrew with babbling tongues, she would forever be a Jew.

A curse lay upon her before she had been born. Her

parents were pipe-liners, promised good money, and told that they could see the world if they'd carve apart the most delicate limbs of the Earth, but all they saw was poverty, narcotic ghettos, ghost towns, and indigenous people attempting to survive in pillaged reservations. Who had cursed them, those that called the land home before it had been colonized, the G-d they were abandoning for money, or had they done it to themselves?

Her first home burned to the ground when she was five. It was a dream home built by her parent's hands, with luxurious furniture, three stories high, five bedrooms, two hundred acres of apple trees, and gardens filled with goats. Then, one day, they received a call while working on a pipeline near a reservation in Wyoming, and all of it was gone. Not a single speck of their belongings had been preserved. Every acre of land, every goat, all erased from existence. Several years later, they'd finish another house, equally as large and gorgeous. It would also be tragically destroyed. Here is her first memory: she's staring out of the back of a pickup truck as her mother is driving over a hundred miles per hour on the highway, and there's a twister, spirals of chrome and jet black, eating the cornfields a half-mile away. They make it back to the house in time to get all the dogs and pups in the back of the truck and drive off to northeast Iowa, where the Orthodox family members live. None of them loaned them any money out of fear that the curse could carry onto them.

What was the purpose of owning a house, or anything, she constantly philosophized, if they spent more of their time in other states, living in a motel room, or within a mobile home? Having lost every-

-thing repeatedly, she held no emotions toward clothes or jewelry. The only things she would never let burn in a fire were her cassette tapes and a Walkman. And then, her parents found them, and the one thing she loved and saved money for became a jumbled pile of shattered plastic and knots of magnetic film.

Everything had been deemed a lie to others until she attempted to kill herself to drive out the rage of wanting to kill her own parents. And then it was only half a lie. In sixteen years, she had lived in over thirty states in America, always the new girl at each school, made friends and enemies, and a few months later, she would be forced to rewrite the script. Her parents pretended that it didn't make sense or that they didn't see it coming, and then it happened, and nothing really changed because to be a parent means not to know what should have been done in those detrimental moments until the child has become an adult and hates you forever and then it's too late for apologies to heal anything

The only person that understood was her cousin, Noah. When her parents were away, Noah would take care of the goats, vacuum, dust the house weekly, mow the grass, and tend to the gardens. The two of them would listen to Metallica records in her bed, repeatedly watch The Goonies on a ruined tape, and he'd ask her questions about life outside of the town, daydreaming that they could someday explore it together. She knew that she would have only felt guilt for him if she had died that day that she leaped. 'Nothing Else Matters' by Metallica was on the radio, and she promised him that after she could escape the wretched frozen shithole state, she'd take him with her and save him, no matter the cost. You're like a brother to me, not a cousin, she would proclaim. Blood means nothing. We are of the same soul. You feel the same way that I do when James Hetfield sings with vengeful spite and when the frenetic guitar frets into its epic and melodic solo toward the end. Together, we're the sound that goes on forever.

Around the same time she had thrown herself off the rooftop of a school and survived, someone else was much less fortunate. The boy wasn't related to her, nor did he live in the same town, but it would affect her in ways she was yet to realize. Her town and others around it were so small that they were like a community of organs that needed each other to survive. Most of her friends lived in Harling, where the boy once lived.

T is in the middle seat at the back of the car when another vehicle collides into him and his friends. He flies a great distance out of the window and into a ditch, chunks of glass pierced through his fur, and his head cracked like an egg spilling yolk. Unrecognizable, no, that can't be T, he was such a handsome coyote, how could someone as giving and virginal die in such a brutal way? Aerosmith's 'Dream On' played at the funeral, and anyone that went would be haunted by that song for the rest of their lives. Nobody would ever see his face again, as it would have cost too much to reconstruct his body for an open casket funeral, and then others would know that whatever had been inside of that chestnut box was a fucking mess of skewered brain and flesh and guts bound to be crushed by a mound of dirt. Yet his name would live on.

Word of his death reached her from friends. Her parents read about it in the local newspaper. A few months later, she would meet his best friend, a gray wolf, and they would fall for each other. Her parents would find out that she had gotten pregnant with a Catholic who's four years older than her and throw her out so that she would be forced to live in his car. She would be working at a diner the moment she'd feel the first contractions, and once the baby had been born, they would name it after the dead coyote so that he could live again. What a beautiful sentiment, they will have thought. And then the boy will have memories of dying in a car crash and forever hate them for it, thinking (and not questioning how he'd phrase it), 'Why would you raise me as a Jew with this stupid Christian name? And every time I hear it, I think of him and how he died because that's all I know about him and not of my own fake accidental existence. You cursed me. I'll always hate my name. Hate my face. Hate my everything. And I'll always hate the two of you.'

She will be back home soon, sometime in October, when this scorched land with all its locusts and steaming cow and pig shit and humidity and ravenous thunderstorms and tornado warnings has been interchanged for a calloused fist of slush and snow and brittle air that only gets thinner and brisker with each day. You will confide everything in her, and she will promise to take you to a music festival where Metallica plays last on the center stage. But for now, you'll have to spend most days walking up and downhill to detassel corn by hand.

Across from your cousin's empty home is your grandmother's house, where she takes care of her daughter, Efa, that had been dually diagnosed with cerebral palsy and Down syndrome. You and other family members would frequently visit to help with chores around the house and gardens and give Efa the attention she deserved. While you'd thumb the piano or improvise with an accordion, Efa would laugh excitedly and sometimes cry, but most of the time doze off and sleep and grandmother would quilt and watch baseball beside you. Everyone made sure always to invite your grandma to any family gathering, and so Efa would come with as well, carried in her wheelchair to the flooded muddy creeks, the open pasture when fireworks were shot into the open sky, and to every Shabbat and holiday service.

What you would give to have your cousin with you right here and now, where she would braid Efa's hair, and you'd file and paint her nails. Away from that house filled with all of its maniacal screaming, slamming doors, carnage, nails splintering through the floorboards, and centipedes wriggling through moldy holes in the walls. What constitutes home seems only to conjure more demons and poltergeists as time goes on, whereas, in grandmother's house, G-d is reputably ever-present with love and forgiveness. But healing is never permanent, whether the body is already broken and crumbling or young and flourishing. Someday, this home known as your heaven would be leveled for the construction of a slaughterhouse, Efa would die before her own mother, your grandmother would die after losing her parents and many more of her children, and you, too, would also have to die. All that would be left are the fragments of decomposing memories of these holy people that weren't enough to preserve you through this world's curse of endless hate and violence.

Had it been fog or the cosmic stardust of angels that filled your bedroom as you tip-toed to the open window and gazed out at the moon over the hills where your father had been dismantling a tractor and reassembling it with new parts? And your sister, on the other side of the pebble-colored walls, her head buried in a pillow with stork feathers in her crusted ebony hair. Screaming for G-d to make the pain stop, and her speaking as if G-d had just responded back to her. Voices not hers, faint, elsewhere, beneath the floorboards, and inside the empty attic. You adjusted your glasses, headed out into the hallway, inhaling the scent of a coming storm, and brushed open your sister's bedroom door with one paw. "Sister. It's me, Noah." You half-smiled and felt guilt in your stomach, for you hated how seeing her like this made you want to cry, even though her illness was beyond anyone's control. "Can I?" The springs in the bed screeched like high-pitched violin strings as you sat beside her on the bed. She coiled beside you, her head nuzzled your thigh, and she nodded. The front door slammed and rattled the entire house. You licked your lips, then the reed, and lullabied the voices, memories, and her brain of visceral mush to a blissful rest.

When they found your sister on the side of the road, she'd been caked with blood from head to toes, un-

-conscious, and barely breathing. It would be days before they could bring her out of a coma. Even though she could still speak, her words would never mean anything ever again. She spoke of monsters, demons, ghosts, death, killing, being killed, raped, then laughter always before the screaming. The LSD she had taken, whether by choice or force, had permanently altered her brain. What she had felt and witnessed when her mind slipped into that altered state would be her new reality.

In a town as small as yours, word of anything spreads like a twister. Someone could have seen you get yelled at by your parents at the grocery store, and by the end of the day, half of the town would have already gossiped about it. But what had happened to your sister, everyone would know, but nobody would speak of it. How could anyone know who could have done it when violence was so common under the roof of almost every house? She was a mirror out in the open to what was meant to be hidden and silenced. Now everybody had known their own evil.

For half of her day, she would have a sense of dream-like clarity but couldn't speak and wandered the house and yards of corn like an infant seeing the world for the first time. But for the rest of the day, she could only cope with the memories by hiding under her bed-sheets and freezing into a state of catatonia.

While you were hunched over and milking one of the many cows, Riley stopped behind you with a bucket in each of his hands and gazed down upon you. You were a thirteen-year-old fox boy whose family immigrated from Poland in the late 1930s to escape the Holocaust, and he was a seventeen-year-old gray wolf boy whose family came from Germany in the 1890s when they realized farming in America presented more opportunity than wherever they had been doing their brickmaking beforehand. What you'd always recognized were his frothy storm clouds of fur, but outside of the barn, you fantasized of the pure white hidden under his shirt and ragged denim overalls. You weren't so young and naïve to know that he didn't have an interest in you, too.

Riley kneeled to put the milk buckets down and then asked pleasantly, "Has anyone told you that you have the most beautiful tail? I hope you don't find it weird for me to say it. I'm not a queer or anything if that's what you're worried about."

You dragged one full bucket next to the others, thought to fill the next, but went against it and stood up to face the much taller wolf. Instinctively, your bushy beige and amber tail quivered as heat and embarrassment flustered in your belly. Other boys would have felt pressured to physically fight back against such a wanton statement. However, you simply reassured him, "It wouldn't bother me if you were queer. People always tell me that my tail is pretty, but I never know what to say about it. I guess that I don't like compliments. It'd be better if people said I was ugly or said nothing because… What does it matter anyway?"

He moved closer to you and rested one paw on your shoulder, and even as he leaned forward, he was still more than a foot taller than your flimsy four-foot-nine height. Drool and spit drizzled from his teeth as his snout barely opened to form a surprised smile.

"You're queer, aren't you, Noah?" He waited for the boy to answer. Once Noah shook his head, he turned his face away in fear of disappointment. "Either way, whether you believe it or not, you're still beautiful in my eyes. You shouldn't hate yourself... All because you feel different. Maybe others strangely look at you because of that thing between your ears, but I think that hat is the cutest thing ever."

Before he left the barn with his hands once again full, this time with jugs of milk, he boasted with glee, "I lied. I'm queer, too. You're too scared of me to tell a soul, and you should be. It's not safe to be a fairy in the town unless you want to die, or worse. Keep my secret, and I'll keep yours. And if you ever have questions about it, I can help you out. I'll always be your friend, Noah."

You pulled yourself upward under the bedsheets and pulled hard at your cock as if you were milking the cows in front of Riley, but like every other time before, you never looked under to see what you were doing to yourself. If it had been thoughts of a woman, you were sure you'd glamor in the glee of masturbation, but this had to be hidden, even from yourself, as much as possible. "I'm not a queer," you'd sometimes grunt with conviction in front of a mirror by your dresser. But there you were, pulling back and forth as rough as possible to the idea of two deer you knew a few grades above you, their mouths conjoined, and their cocks against one another. And you thought of what it might look like when you'd return to school and attempt to hide your erection under a towel in the locker room until you'd find a corner for yourself in the shower room. Then, in your melted mind, Riley slowly removed his denim overalls to reveal that chest of puffy white fur.

Sister had begun her abrupt high-pitched scream that sounded like she had just been confronted by the longest and sharpest knife imaginable. When your hand fell back in defeat and horror, it felt for the clarinet. It wasn't her fault, but you felt like punishing her. You would rather let her suffer the memories of what happened that night instead of playing her Hashkiveinu for the thousandth time.

There were two empty seats at the dinner table, one reserved for your dead brother and the other for your older sister, who had been stomping above your heads. Your father clawed apart a whole roasted chicken and placed it beside the rice and baked vegetables to the left of your plate. All you could see was the animal that it once was before it was beheaded, feathered, and skinned, the moment when it ran across the yard with blood spurting from its neck before it fell flat behind the truck. Now it was on your plate, releasing a mess of juices over Hebrew inscriptions, burnt and hacked apart.

A vision came to mind of you standing upon cotton white clouds, donning a halo that vibrated with a concerning hum. Before you, there were thousands of animals, along with bugs of all kinds. G-d had de-

-manded you to kneel and ask for their forgiveness and explain why you thought it was vital for them to die for your convenience.

"Is it true that the Nazis would cut off our tails and shave us before putting us in the gas chamber," you asked, even though you wholeheartedly knew the answer. "That there are exhibits that have mountains of our tails and fur? I heard that they would sometimes feed us to the guard dogs, so it was easier to break us into pieces before stuffing us into the crematories."

Your mother continued to focus on filling her plate, refused to look you in the eyes, although she maintained an outlandish gawk, and asked in bewilderment, "Why are you asking about this, Noah? Your father has been working morning to night every day of the week, and it's our time to rest. And I haven't had a day off from the hardware store in almost a month. Why do you have to be such a strange child, Noah?"

"This isn't right. I won't eat this. We're animals, too. What if someone decided that we foxes aren't that intelligent after all, and then we're suddenly produced like livestock and slaughtered? Some people eat elk in this country. Look north of the state! A third of our family is elk! It's not so unreasonable to ask these sorts of questions. I don't want my body to be a cemetery any longer."

"Eat the fucker, damn you!" Your father slammed the table with his fist and pointed a finger in your direction. "If I have to take this belt off and whack your ass and your back all fucking night until I see blood, then I'll do it. You're nothing but a spoiled brat. That's what it sounds like to me." He banged the table once again. Sister must have heard it because she was screaming even louder now. "Now look what you've done, fucking shithead. Be grateful you're sitting where you are now and not where your sister is. Your life could be a hell of a lot worse. You could have been gassed in a damn camp. Or shot to death with your dad before your mother was stripped and raped. Do you know how badly we starved when we came to this country before suffering for all of this land? And you won't eat what I killed, what your mother cooked, and what G-d has given to you?"

Somehow, the fear hadn't resonated, and you continued to argue, "G-d wouldn't want us to kill animals like this. Farming is changing, and you know it, too. It's not like it was when you were a teenager."

"We shouldn't take him down to the city anymore," your mother shook her head, albeit speaking calmly. "From now on, we'll keep him here, our Shul in town, far away, removed from those city kids teaching him to become an herbivore. And we shouldn't take him up north either. Who knows what the Orthodox were telling him."

"Every other Jewish family except our own will be gone from this town in ten years, and you know it! There's nothing here for us. A few Jewish families aren't going to keep the Shul running forever. It'll be closed down and redecorated as a church. Better yet, they'll tear it down so that slaughterhouse they want to build can take its place. Everyone wants us out. They want us dead! The Klan even burned down Sarah's home!"

Your father rose from his chair with vehement rage and brought one slap across your face, and a moment later, a belt was in his hand, and you were staggered over the table with your snout rubbing into the plate. He yelled once again, "Eat the fucker, damn you! I said fucking eat it!" Mother came over to stop him, and then she was swaddled to the ground before he was back on top of you. Blood was on the kitchen floor by one leg of the table, along with a broken plate that scattered chicken, rice, and vegetables over your mother's dress. "Start fucking counting off!" You counted. One. Two. The belt whipped higher up on your shoulders. When it hit your tail, you cried louder and imagined your father as some sort of Nazi soldier priming it up for removal. He only stopped with the punishment when his arms grew tired, and the moment you hit the floor beside your mother, you lifted your pants, and the pain was no more. You had won; what he had accomplished didn't matter because you hadn't taken a single bite of the chicken.

Later in the night, after slamming and locking your door and listening to your mother beg to be let in so she could apologize and dress your wounds, which you refused to let her do, you imagined your father coming to the door with three gentle knocks, a murmured voice, and him sitting down beside you as you'd do for your sister almost every night, and his apology resonating in a way more beautiful than any quartet of klezmer music filling a synagogue or outside the house on a birthday night. It would never come. The next day, he would force himself to forget that he had ripped into your fur and left permanent scars, but he'd never dress your plate with chicken or fish again.

A few nights after you were beaten, your sister spoke to you in clarity for the first time in over a month. You'd just finished a fourth song, an improvisation on an accordion, and then she squeezed your arm, dug her eyes into yours, and muttered, "Stars, all over the room. He's here with us now. See?"

Pale orbs the size of chicken eggs were scintillating in the air all over the hickory walls, forming their own kind of moonlight while the mossy green aurora from outside beamed across the cracked wooden floorboard. At first, you found it to be beautiful and comforting, as was your sister's unusual smile, but then you saw a figure by the door, so tall that the back of its head was pressed to the ceiling, and feathery wings spreading across the walls while its hands drooped below its knees. It began to sob and slide closer at a snail's pace, whining, "I'm sorry… I'm sorry… I didn't mean to kill him. I didn't mean to kill myself. I'm sorry… I'm sorry… Don't be scared of me. I don't want to be dead anymore. Please, bring me back. I didn't mean to kill him. I didn't mean to kill myself. I'm sorry… I'm sorry…"

In the blink of an eye, your deceased brother had vanished back to his grave, and you riveted off the bed to the sound of your sister wailing into her wet little wrists. A scream of complete terror. Then her hands all over her nightgown, pulling it, but it wasn't her hands pulling it, and then she threw herself back and forth against the mattress, but it wasn't her doing it, was it? You thought that some invisible entity must be tormenting her. Nothing could be done but to walk out of the room, lock the door, and stare at the drywall until the banging and screaming let up.

There were four in the car, and it's not like snow had been blinding their vision or the roads were icy; it was like any other night in the autumn where there were no streetlights for miles upon dirt roads in the no-where Iowa country. Noah's older brother, Isaac, he'd been driving responsibly, not a lick of alcohol inside of his body, and rambling with the Catholic boy in the passenger seat. The two in the back were wasted from the party, one teen whose name doesn't matter because he lived and nobody knew him or cared about him, and another kid named Riley. All of them except for Isaac were from the same town, and when he saw their car had broken down, he had been willing to give them a lift back home even if it meant being whipped bloody by his dad that night.

"I'm starting to wonder that the world might be evil, that it's going against me, or us, or something," Isaac thought out loud as he tried to navigate through the abyss.

T stuck his hand out of the window and let the cool air breeze against it and tried not to let his mind drift off to shitty hair metal lyrics so that he could make conversation with the older boy. Any other night, he would have disagreed. He was a bright Catholic boy that his parents and siblings loved and looked up to; he confessed at church anytime he did anything that seemed sinful, swore never to drink, smoke, or have sex unless it were after marriage, and never bullied a soul. Like any coyote in the eighties, his hair was longer in the back than the front, which was his defiance from dealing with a standard bowl cut. If it weren't for this day, he would have been going to an Aerosmith concert far away in Minneapolis. Dream on, T. The endless web of dreams that never come true.

"Starting to think I'm cursed," Isaac went on. "I mean, there aren't any signs on the road. It's like we've ventured out into The Twilight Zone. I'm not kidding. Just look!"

There were no signs, and whatever homes existed had their own hills of dirt roads hidden by cornfields. Sometimes, they'd stop at a four-way road with no stop signs, and he would ponder if anything looked familiar or if they were still going in circles.

"Yeah, well, maybe I'm cursed, too," T acknowledged. His right hand made surf waves.

And it was more than likely that he had been. T had also not drunk that night; he wanted to give his friend a ride home, who was half drunk, and felt that it was his duty to provide the thirteen-year-old with a ride, who had drunk more than anyone else at the party. He thought about how he had done no wrong in the past and his parent's reaction to finding out that his car had broken down in a place he couldn't recall while giving two drunks a lift.

Riley dug his palms into his temples, sobbing, groaning between his legs, and holding back vomit. It wasn't only the regret of drinking or the fever, but a different kind of sickness that he felt enraging the core of his being. The conversation only maddened him more, and he thought he might explode and kill everyone in the car.

"Like... It doesn't matter how much you love someone or how messed up a situation seems," Isaac yelled out vaguely but then continued to clarify. "My Grandpa just died, and seeing his face, you know, him dead and shit, it seemed like the biggest joke to me at the hospital. Because, then I saw everyone I know dead like that—their dead faces and shit. The rot, infesting bugs, and the way your chest explodes inside a coffin. You suffer, you hurt, people love you, they want you to live, but then you fucking die. Then there's that dead face that says nothing, and that's it. It's just over, man… Fucking, like, G-d gave us this free will, and we said let's kill everything for power until it kills us. Tell me to stop if I'm going too far or if I offend you. My Grandparents, they escaped the death camps, but there were still these mass murders in villages, where they'd take all of the Jews to an open field or into the woods, shoot them, and bury them in mass graves. I often think about that, about those that didn't survive. You thought you and your family would survive, that the world would overcome this corrosive bigotry, and then, BLAM! Your Christian neighbors turn you in, those who peacefully lived beside you for over two hundred years or something, and they'll get killed, too, but not until you're shot dead with your kids and wife. Tell me that the world isn't evil. Tell me that humans aren't born evil. We're all evil, I think. Even me."

T thought about what he said in silence, listened to the wind and the car's engine more than the radio, and finally answered, "G-d cries with you. It hurts him just as much as it hurts us when these things happen."

"FUUUUUUUUUUUUCCCCK." Riley growled out through his searing migraine. "Just. Shut the fuck up. You're both fucking idiots. And you think you know pain or the worst of everything, but you don't. You're so fucking lucky. Don't even realize it. Just shut the fuck up. Shut the fuck up! My brain. It's a fucking CANCER! A CANCER! And I was fucking born like this? What the fuck did I do to deserve it? None of you know fucking shit about suffering."

"You fucking vomited all over his car, you little shit-faced faggot shit," The boy beside him antagonized. "You're the one that needs to shut the fuck up, you fucking faggot freak fuck."

Isaac looked behind him briefly before turning back to face the road. He shook his head and calmly assured, "It's fine. Like... I lost my train of thought. Well, I have this family member, and she's sick... Everyone loves and takes care of her. She's stuck in this wheelchair, can't speak, and her face isn't normal like ours. It's all, wah, you know? Because she was born with some fuck-story kind of shit. One day, she's gonna die, though. And she's gonna die young. Well, maybe she's as pure as you and me. But maybe that's wrong to say? Insensitive? What are angels, anyway? I think she's my family's angel. Everyone goes to her and my grandmother for guidance, the two most tortured souls, and one of them can't even speak or move two-thirds of their own body. It doesn't matter how many times anyone combs her hair, gives her a sponge bath with bubbles, takes her to shul, or a birthday party. She's going to die, and it's going to be painful and ugly. It isn't fair."

As he was thinking out loud about his cousin, another car speeding from the opposite direction without its headlights on collided directly into theirs. There wasn't enough time for any of them to notice or react from the cosmic pain they'd been forced to indure.

Isaac's neck slammed right into the steering wheel, which instantaneously snapped his neck and killed him, and then he ricocheted into his seat as glass rained through his face. The car twisted once before it continued driving forward and fell right into a ditch. His body slouched forward over the wheel, and a halo appeared over his head as his soul shot right through the sky and toward a nebula shaped like a feline eye.

T had been thrown out of the car upon impact. Miniscule shards of glass had ripped through all of his fur and his bones. Most of the skin from his face had been torn off when his head collided with the road, exposing part of his skull, skewering his eyes, and bludgeoning his cheeks. His limbs were bent out of place and it was as if he'd been captured by a tornado and beaten to a pulp.

While the other unknown boy had only slammed his head against the back seat and went unconscious, Riley had remained awake the entire time. He unbuckled his seat belt and felt nothing when he fell forward against the back of the passenger seat. The car alarm was beeping, toxic fumes and smoke were consuming the vehicle, and he wondered if it would explode. Some good must have existed in him, whether he remembered doing it or not, because he had managed to help the other living boy out of the car and pull him out from the ditch. As he placed him on the side of the road, the vehicle caught on fire and exploded into an inferno alongside the other car.

As he stared, mesmerized by the flames and then by the wretched corpse on the road, he couldn't help but smile maliciously and think, 'That should have been me, and it's not. This world is cursed and evil; it tells me that I deserve you. They say I shouldn't, but I'm going to, anyway. I'm going to love you like a car crash burning out of control, and I won't let go until I've destroyed myself."

"Sometimes, I can see into the lives I have once lived and will live," you elucidated. "A new memory came to light, with a different body. It was strange because he wasn't a Jew. I always thought the magic, or whatever it is, only linked to those related to our family. He was the one driving the car. Riley was there, too. It's all connected, somehow. I'm beginning to think Riley might like me. Maybe, we're going to save and protect each other."

The stone remained unresponsive. You collected branches beside the grave, snapped them over your kneecap, and tossed them aside. Underneath the grass was a plain wooden coffin containing a skeleton consumed with dirt and insects and bound by tree limbs. In front of you were acres of soybeans, hills of tall grass glistening from the sun, ancient oak trees, and three houses in the distance. You stepped to the far end of the cemetery and removed a plastic bag with tefillin from your backpack. Here is the only place where time is nonexistent. You prayed with your eyes closed, davening with the embrace of the wind and its song, a quintillion of angels upon your shoulders, held the heart of the sun, and were blinded by it at the end of your prayer. Some other day but not yet, you'd bury it all right there. The prayer shawl, torn in half, tefillin in knots, cremated prayer books. And then you would return to it again, many decades later, after most of your family had been nailed into their own caskets.

On the way home, while walking in the dirt with one hand brushing through the corn, you glanced upward to the twitch in your ears and noticed a young coyote standing naked in the middle of the road. He appeared lost, not feral, but not like you, either. Like he had lost all sense of identity and memories. There was a broken innocence in his ebony eyes, which he had been sniffing around for somewhere in the gravel. You guessed that he must have been your age, so you called out to him, "Hey! You from around here?" There was no response. The second you stepped onto the road, it felt like your feet were crunching bones and sinking into blood. The coyote looked back and acknowledged you for a moment as if to say hello in a sheepish way, and then it vanished to the other side, up and over the hill, one that you knew led nowhere for miles. By the time you reached the top, the coyote was gone as if it had disintegrated. The only places that existed were half a mile away; there had been a set of abandoned homes once owned by Jews that left the city, a Catholic cemetery, and a grain factory. At that moment, as out of focus and blurry in monochrome as it had been, you realized who the boy was and prayed that he'd find his way back.

"What if he saw me because I'm a ghost, too," you whispered to your dead brother. There was no response, not even a wisp of wind to signal that he heard or even existed as an angel. Then you thought, maybe there are no angels, and all that becomes of the body is the slow rot into a nest of dirt and insects or a wandering soul permanently caged in its own hell. "Born a ghost. Born dead. Born cursed."

Here is the road where your brother and the other boy had been killed. Where they also must have found your older sister barely breathing. And then there was the other girl you went to school with but never talked to because she wasn't a Jew, who was last seen with a stranger in a truck by the same street sign you stood under. You would never forget her bruised eyes, unkempt dresses, and snout dug into her desk every day. These tragedies would eventually be ignored by the townsfolk and those that'd leave, but not you. Those that would choose to forget would be reminded of it, two decades later, with the blood of pigs and cows and even elk that would flood this road. You saw it in your dreams and felt it in your heart. Maybe G-d had once existed in all parts of the world, but not anymore, and certainly not here.

Summer would soon be over, which entailed the momentary autumn that'd inevitably be crushed by blizzards six months of sunless tombstone skies. At this time every year, other relatives that lived in different parts of Iowa and Nebraska would visit, always two weeks before school started back up again. Along with continual farm work and monotonous chores, now there would be cousins taking your bed while you slept in a bag on the floor. It was custom to sing and perform songs from most evenings until midnight, both ancient and new, always religious, and done in Hebrew. Other Jewish neighbors would also visit and observe the musical performances and pass around bottles of wine while most of the kids played basketball inside of the garage or retreated to the barn to throw around pornographic magazines and smoke cigarettes and talk about sports and girls (even in front of the girls).

For a while, it felt like your sister had joined your brother. Nobody other than you passed by her room or checked in to ensure she ate her food. Otherwise, her name was not even mentioned in a single conversation.

None of the others knew as many instruments as you did. The others would whisper behind their hands to your parents to remind them how proud they were of you, how they hoped you could leave this town and someday see your full potential. Your parents would nod but never respond. They'd gaze and admire your talent but refuse to accept it. One child was already dead, another was practically in a walking coma, and the third had become a conceited brat. All their eyes were upon you but unable to hear what you wanted them to know. Their prayers were sterile and redundant. Hadn't they gotten all they needed and been given the glory to relish in it all by now? You had everything in the world and more to pray for, and G-d seemed deaf to your resonant melodies. When you pressed onto the keys of your accordion, you always hoped that she knew that you played for her and not for them.

A few days after the house had been packed with relatives, your cousin finally made it home and came to visit you. You were wearing a The Police band shirt and black swim trunks, dancing with your sister, while your cousin organized jewelry on the bed, and it was turning out to be the best day of your life. While the two of you listened to records in your sister's room, your parents and hers argued downstairs about the fate of everything. *You can't raise a girl like that. Of course she wants to kill herself. You've been holding her hostage with your job ssince she was born. Both of you were high-class fuckups, and then you beat her when she did the same as you. Either way, I don't want her around Noah anymore. Fix your coke-head daughter, buy some farmland, and stop being victims to your bullshit.* Sarah confesses that she's already met someone in town, a farmer boy from a Catholic family, and tells you how wonderful he is. If she didn't have to leave until winter, maybe she could find a way to stay here with him and leave her parents behind. *Yeah, just tear this entire family apart while you're at it. You and your husband are so fucking delusional. Us Jews aren't meant to be living here; there's no future here for any of us. G-d knows that I certainly don't want to be here. They've already burned down our house once, right after we had built it from scratch after the tornado. Telling your kid to take over the farm isn't a gift. If you want him to be an observant Jew, the best thing you can do is set him free.*

You and the other children made ditches in the mud down by the lake. Great grandmother was by the picnic table with Efa in the wheelchair, and your cousin Sarah smoked cigarettes with the water to her knees. Cousins, all elk and Orthodox, twisted you around in the mud while you playfully pushed them down and sometimes held them underwater. Your thick coat of clementine orange would remain wet for only a brief second before the sun simmered the molecules away, visible rays of steam rising from your soul. Steam dazzled off threads and disintegrated above your flickering ears. In your Grandma's eyes was the portrait she had survived to see completed. Here, where you'd been born. Clawing further with both hands, you reached for an umbilical cord or lifeline. Instead, you found the root from some tree, and when you pierced it, the Catholic boy from the car crash dream came to mind.

The other boys staying in your room were outside throwing baseballs while you had a chair to your doorknob, a sock in one hand, and the other sock around your dick. There were faces drawn and colored with sharpie markers on both socks, fox and wolf, googly eyes drooping with globs of glue where two toes on opposite ends would normally be. Riley was on you with a loose embrace. As you got close, you stuffed the one you weren't using into your mouth so nobody in the house could hear. If Riley could find out and also prove that he actually liked you. When you ejaculated, your imagination of Riley distorted into something else, him in a ditch at night, his body on fire, melting into the wet grass, and there was a hole the size of a fist in the back of his head with a candlelight dancing inside of it. The chair rattled and jolted toward the bedframe as both boys raced in and barely gave you enough time to hide under the sheets to pretend like you were trying to rest. As they jumped onto the bed and begged you to go back out and play, you slipped the socks back on, never mind the mess in one of them, and promised to join them. Instead, you went back to sleep, easing the lazy days that you couldn't be with him to waste.

While you were busy making the cum socks kiss, Riley had been babysitting a six-year-old boy a few houses down. There might have been times when he left the house to walk around the mailbox, to see if any other kids were running along the hills, and maybe to listen closely for an accordion, but mostly, his eyes were on the TV and on the boy beside him on the sofa. It wasn't like his hands were caressing or manipulating anything; they just rested there because that's what he preferred doing most with a boy. Doing anything more would be too much. If he got carried away, he knew he wouldn't be able to stop. Once every two weeks, maybe, that's perfect, especially if they were young enough to forget or too innocent to understand what he was even doing. The delusions he designed while imagining the car on fire and himself in the ditch. He'd think, 'It's not like I'm hurting them. I'm not a fucking serial killer. Nobody could ever understand this - my love surpasses all others.'

Here's what Riley was thinking about while he sat in the car's passenger seat before it transformed into a hearse on fire. Just one memory from six years ago and no more unique than the others. Riley walked out of the barn while his father was screaming at workers about spilled paint and how important it was for everyone in the town to know they were the only dairy farm in the area to be Grade A. He could see his mother blankly watching TV and knitting through the cyan screen door. After he tossed off his muddy boots near the front door, he ate his morning porridge beside her and stood up at the cross situated over a picture frame of him and his parents. His paws were bruised and bloody from raking hay and scooping shit from the previous night and that morning. He wanted to pray aloud to Jesus, but he'd be as good as dead if his mom heard what he had to say. When his dad came in, he was already spitting on the carpet, kicking and punching holes in the wall, and talking about how he should have never left Wisconsin to come to Iowa. He spoke about how he could have made more and had a better family back home as he ate his breakfast in the kitchen. And so she stopped knitting, listened, but said nothing, hoping that his anger would snuff out like a candle flame. The oatmeal was cold, so he threw half of it across the kitchen and moved aggressively to the living room as if he were ready to attack her again. Riley felt her grip on his shoulders and stiffened as he blanketed her chest and most of her face. With a disgusted look, his dad froze in awe and taunted, "You'd use our son as a shield for what you deserve? And I'm the bad parent? Telling me, look what you've done, and shit. Yet you'd hide behind him instead of throwing him out of the way and accepting my fist? Only thinking for yourself. Just like any other woman. After killing two of our babies, you'd do that to my only child. If I could, I swear that I would kill you. Nothing would make me happier. You'd make me hurt my fucking son to get to you?"

Riley wrestled himself out his mother's grip until he could scramble away from her on the floor. Slowly, he got up, and as he looked away, he decided he'd never protect her again, even as she called out for help. He carefully walked to his bedroom and attempted to dissociate from the sounds of her being beaten and raped again

Later that day, his father would come to his room after school, one hand nuzzling his ears and the other on a blanket over his stomach, and tell him how sorry he was while he stared at the cross in his bedroom. Everyone was always so fucking sorry, yet they couldn't stop hurting each other. He cried to Jesus and begged that he'd never be corrupted. That he'd never hurt someone else. And then one day his face slammed against the driver's seat, and the music went out.

Riley took you for a drive out of town. An hour and a half passed by before you had seen anything other than the low hills among cornfields, an endless boring array of emerald and daffodil that you sometimes believed were all that existed in the world, and everything else was a lie.

You'd ask nothing but questions as if he were the thickest open book. "And your parents let you drive wherever you want, whenever you want? Do they not care about you? Can you take me there? Can you show me your favorite hidden places? Are you sure we can do it all in one day? Aren't you ever scared of people from the city? Can we see a movie? Can you take me to the record store? Why do you like The Cure so much?"

He took a long way around to show you where he thought you'd find the most intriguing. There were two synagogues in Omaha, Nebraska, and you knew that many people that once lived in your town were now going there for services. He parked the car for a few minutes so that you could see people leaving Shabbat services, but you couldn't recognize anyone. Then he drove to the university's library and answered most of your questions that he previously stalled on while he finished a pack of cigarettes. Yes, they let him drive whenever he wanted, wherever he wanted. No, they didn't care about him. Yes, he could take you to every secret hiking trail, every bench under a hill near a graveyard, and every record store. It would take more than a day, but he said it would give him another excuse to go into the city. There were theaters, but he had other ideas. He'd buy you three records. Because The Cure finds beauty in heartbreak.

"You should go to school here," he encouraged with gleeful eyes. "The shul is close by, and you have gay bars, tons of jobs, cheap apartments… The farm isn't in your blood. You're better than that. I'd be sad to see a cute queer like you forced to marry and have kids and break your body doing the kind of work that isn't meant for you. I bet you'd find someone nice, like some kind of rich doctor."

But you had thought that--, and you almost said it, but then you quickly knew it wasn't. Instead, you asked, "What about you? Are you gonna move here the second you can escape your parents?"

"No, no." He sat back up and threw his cigarette out of the window. "This place isn't meant for me. I want to move somewhere that never gets snow or below forty degrees. Not sure how yet, or where exactly. But. We'll see."

You wondered what you meant to him. He took you down to the city, thought of you the whole ride, and wanted to show you all of these things, cement this moment into your memory, but refused to say that he loved you. But he must have, right? At any second, which had never come.

Later that night, he let you pick a movie, and even though he hated Star Wars, he assured you that it was okay because it was with you, and who knows, maybe he would learn to change his perspective and enjoy it differently. The house was quiet, and it's almost like his mom wasn't trying to wash off bruises that weren't there anymore or like his dad wouldn't come home drunk to pass out naked on the sofa. The two of you cuddled in front of the glowing chrome tube, and as you wished that either of you would drift asleep in less than underwear, it never happened. He wouldn't even allow himself to kiss your forehead or along your shoulders. Even so, at that moment, you believed that if that were the only romantic experience you'd ever have with a man for the rest of your life, you'd accept it with grace.

"Rest with me here."

It was dawn with the drone of the frogs and cicadas singing. You'd both gone through the Jewish cemetery, over the gate, and rolled out a blanket on the downslope of the hill so you could face the stars. The longer you stared, the more you could imagine that the galaxy had fallen into the cornfields.

On a previous fourth of July, you, Sarah, and a few others had been invited to the Ark's farmhouse, in which they exploded thousands of dollars worth of fireworks. Rob had a telescope pointed out from the top floor of a barn that appeared to focus on nothing in particular, but once you gazed through, there was a crimson stardust lagoon. How you hoped to own a telescope of your own someday, or become one, venturing into space, taking photographs for the Earth, maybe evaporating into something others thought was a nebula, but in fact, is the eye of G-d.

"I bet you come out here a lot," Riley surmised. "Guess I would, too. All I ever do is hide in my room with a pillow over my face. At day, to the lake, so you become one with the state. An Iowa cub. At night, to be close with your brother."

Between the two of you was a clarinet. Dad knew how to play it better than you and your sister preferred when you used the accordion. Sitting up, tail swaying, you licked the reed and practiced a few melodies for him that felt like failures to you but were the most profound things he'd heard. Others in town, even Sarah, their taste in music was shit.

You ranted and proclaimed, "People outside the Midwest from the cities think this land is flat, monotonous, ugly. Yet all they see is metal, hot glass, concrete, advertisements of an artificial world. The sky is a black ceiling to them. There is no G-d, only money and politics. Here, I can practice songs as loud as I want at night, and only the dead will hear me. I have everything I need right here. Even when the work is tough, and it takes hours to get the grime out from my fur, I can come here, stargazing on the blanket I was born on, right beside the person I like most."

As you told him stories of your ventures in solitude, he curled up on one side and tried to imagine what you might look like nude, something he was sure he'd never see. The infinite stars that brought you awe and gave you meaning brought the opposite out of him. He closed his eyes as he spoke harshly and honestly, "Personally, I fucking hate this place. You'll learn to hate it just as much as I do if a small piece of you doesn't already."

After you fell asleep, he thought to do the same beside you but reasoned against it, in fear that someone
might visit the graves in the morning and find two
queers bound together. Your dream was constructed
from the name Riley had given you - Iowa cub. In it,
you'd found the thick, muddy canal by the lake you'd
built with your elk cousins and leaped headfirst into it.
The mud sucked you up, and you swayed through the
murky water, gazing at branches as leaves bloomed
and decayed and limbs croaked from the weight of
snow. When you exited the water, spirits maundered
the forests. Their bodies were like thin black cloaks
with moons for eyes. One of them was surely your
brother.

There were entities other than the ghosts that seemed
to have found themselves just as lost as you. The wolf-
fox you'd seen before dug his paws into the dirt behind a tree while a familiar coyote hunched over him
with his hands pressed to his chest. As the cub wept,
the teen above attempted to speak, but no words
could come out. Furthermore, his body was in a state
of continuously evaporating and regenerating, like
TV static. You knelt beside him and started digging as
well, unsure of what you'd recover.

Eventually, he gave up digging and exclaimed, "At the
end of my light, I had this vision, and even though you
weren't in it, I know you're a part of it, just like him
that can't speak to me. I don't know anything about
him, except for his name and death. Yet here we are.
There's supposed to be more than this. But I think it's
time I stop digging and begin to wander like them."

Sarah was so in love and her gut twisted like the tornado that ravaged her second house, and she knew destruction would come of it, but she took his hand and continued to follow him through the carnival. They could hear the revving engines of the monster truck show, rifles shooting glass bottles, infants screaming, and wolf boys howling, and they knew this would be a day that'd stop her from ever wanting to jump off of a rooftop again. He was a few years older and from a Catholic family and a different species and a bad boy with an empathetic but sick heart, and they just got back from a Def Leppard concert and sang every song lyric in unison, and after the encore, that's when they both realized that together, they would be connected forever.

"Your place is like a dollhouse. I've never seen anything like it," Rob laughed as he tried to focus on random thoughts bouncing in his head. "The strawberry wallpaper, those violet curtains caked in dust. And your dad, with his cowboy hat, Marlboro cigarettes, the talking fish on the kitchen wall... It's not what I'd expect from a Jewish family. My family's Catholic, but I don't think they believe in any of it. They just do it to look good to the other families we're related to and the rest of the town. Maybe it's the same for you. Ah, damn, and the apple honey tea in your New York City coffee cup. That, too. I mean, I've never played with dolls or anything. Sorry. You're having a good day, right?"

The Ferris Wheel had a maintenance issue while the two were stuck at the top and gazing over the other rides. You could tell each family farm apart from that high, even if most looked the same. His was the largest, the most expansive, and it would always be that way. He's an Ark, which meant that before she was born, the blood in his family had been the reason her and most of your family were alive. She hoped that someday, she could be an Ark, too. As her hand squeezed him, she tried to imagine what his eyes or mind were focusing on. What if it were the winding road, its hills, and the four-way stop where his best friend died? She'd been told that he and T were nearly identical, except that he didn't believe in a G-d, while his friend was the most spiritual and practicing person he knew. In other words, he was T in a world of G-d being dead.

Knowing her mind was racing, he asked, "What are you thinking about?"

"What am I thinking about? I'm thinking, 'what are you thinking about?'"

"I'm thinking…."

He didn't know how to explain it, so he took her right paw, lifted it under his shirt, and placed it over his heart, which had a lump over it that made a ticking sound. The ride started back up, and they were slowly being gyrated back down to the bottom. What he saw in her eyes, knowing she'd be there for every surgery, just like his mother had been there for the first one he had at the age of eight. Between synapses, memories of collapsing into a pool of his own blood as a kid, how many times he was meant to die, but instead others went into flames, and could it all be so that he would find her, heart like a Ferris Wheel, built, broken, fixed again, the two of them speeding down the freeway hundreds of miles away, tails wagging gaily, sitting beside each other on chrome seats outside of a

Cowboys football game, they're gonna win the series, dew of sweat and humid Midwest Iowa in August, treefrogs and cicada's eternal liturgy, the tick tick tick tick tick tick tick of the pacemaker. They kissed, and the rest would be history.

A sunset split through the fog over a baseball field. A boy leaned into the bleachers behind him, stretched out, and faced an ocean in the sky. He used one claw to dig out his face from a Polaroid. And then it was the sound of tractors outside his window before the alarm clock went off. Swimming through the flooded meadows where he had been born. His toes still digging into dirt to form a tunnel to another world in which he never existed. It was the whistle of the cornfields at night and the eyeless albino horses eating maggots inside the basement. The weather might have been too calm, and instead of interpreting it as nirvana or harmony, the stagnant air would bring fear of another tornado. It couldn't last, even if nothing is predestined, which was just as horrifying to contemplate.

Sarah shifted the sheets away as she felt like she was being suffocated by them and hesitantly asked, "Can I tell you something crazy and have you act completely unphased the whole time during the conversation?"

Rob chuckled, reached over to rub her right arm, and responded faintly, "Of course." He thought it was ridiculous that she requested him to act a certain way because he was sure that his closeness with death throughout his life desensitized him to anything oth-

-ers might deem abnormal.

And so she went on to divulge her tale as he brushed her arm, "I saw something outside of the house last night; it came out of the crops, glared right back at me, and vanished just as quickly. But even though it only lasted seconds, the vision pervaded me. It followed me into my dreams, where I was wandering through a forest and searching for him. Suddenly, I felt this intense hum like a bang, throttling me to the ground. It felt like one of my migraines, power drills digging into my eyes, at my temples. Then I saw him in front of me, his head tilted, a black muzzle with streaks of white around his emerald eyes, and his tail was long, broad, and as orange as mine. The second I realized that this half-wolf-half-fox creature was our son, it leaped forward and tore apart my throat, and for some reason, I felt... I felt like I deserved it. For things I haven't done yet."

He squeezed her shoulders and tried to capture the image she had just painted for him. The violence went over his head as he focused on the idea of himself as a father, one unlike his own, a sociopathic alcoholic, and his reassuring grin twisted into a genuine smile. If they had a kid, he'd hope it would be more wolf than a fox, a boy that resembled his own masculinity, that the first thing he'd wear is a Dallas Cowboys onesie, and that the boy would play baseball and maybe football in middle school and not have the same heart issue that he would deal with his entire life and also what if he died during open-heart surgery and left the boy in the hands of a widowed mother still dealing with so much trauma from her own childhood and how hopeless and pointless all of that struggle would be but it wouldn't happen because he already had a plan to get the two of them out of Iowa and after that everything would come naturally.

"None of that is crazy to me." He shrugged and ran his hands through her tail as it fluttered quietly in his lap. "Do you think… Maybe you dreamed of this son killing you because you're afraid of being a bad mother? I think that's a good thing. It means you'd care. You'd do your best and try. Do you know why I think you'd be a good mother? Nobody would care more about keeping their child safe from the shit you went through than you. You know what can happen to kids. And you've got a heart of gold. Even if we were poor our whole lives, you'd spoil him with love. I just know."

Sarah didn't know that Rob also had a dream of the wolf-fox cub, the predestined future son. The boy was resting on his chest while they were watching a science fiction TV show, listening to the tick of his pacemaker, its tick tick tick. As the cub's ears twitched along the surgical scar on Rob's chest, he whispered to him, "Why can't it last forever, daddy? Can't they make better ones, so they don't have to cut you open all the time? It isn't fair. I pray that it ticks until the Earth is no more. If I died right now, could I give you my heart?"

While Rob was in a coma at the mere age of eight, he dreamt that his mother was outside in the hospital's hallway with her head buried between her legs. There was soil stuck under her nails, which she had dug into the back collar of her shirt, and then it was the echo of her bawling helplessly, imagining what it'd be like to see her first son dead before she'd even turn thirty. In the dreamscape, it was Mars orange outside, apocalyptic clementine, and cyclones were ravaging Iowa. His father wasn't present. He wouldn't be there for any of the other surgeries either. Not like his mother. That he hated despite her indestructible love for him. That he hated when people cried over him, reminding him of his irreversible disease, some 'cosmic fuckery'. Rob wasn't in that coma anymore, but the dream had been omnipresent in each breath. He closes his eyes and feels like an expanding sun. Mass ejection to engulf the galaxy.

When he first told Sarah about his heart, he exhorted, "DNA is everything. Only the ones unfortunate enough to be born with something meant to kill them will understand this." In other words, why he ached to be placed in a cryogenic tank, or that he dreamt of 3D printed organs replacing and rebirthing every fragment of his body. Or having not ever existed at all. His Catholic mother and others would preach to him that everything happens for a reason, how it was motivational that he could push through everything, and that he wouldn't be as intelligent or successful if it weren't for it, like it was some wonderful journey to have a terminal heart condition, and how he should never lose hope.

While mother prepared the table, you paced near the door to the laundry room, dazing in and out of reality, imagining yourself in Riley's muddy arms, smelling more like swine than a wolf, but nude this time, wrapped in the Star Wars blanket. The thoughts de-materialized within the rattling cabinets, and doors aggressively opened and closed independently. It was as if the house was in the constant grip of an invisible tornado, tactfully peeling apart the wallpaper and dismantling the frail sodden walls. The storm was over, a short-lived sun shower that had skewed the sky into rays of vermillion and lavender, and yet water continued to drop into bowls across the kitchen. As your eyes peered at a figure down the hall and near your parent's bedroom, your mother pressed a bowl of soup to your chest, which you would have dropped if she hadn't said your name beforehand. For your sister. Cold soup that looked like nasal blood and tasted like dirt.

The house went from mid-seizure to paralyzed as you carefully went up the creaking steps and damaged floorboards. It was the mildew stench of the floral rug. It was the dust-caked across the Magen David painting on one side of the hallway. It was the phantom grip over your restless foot paws. It felt as if whatever you saw downstairs was enveloping you. Inside her bedroom, there was no sister, only the sheets folded with the pillows symmetrically arranged, your accordion at the center of the bed, and the window wide open with the screen missing. The sound of the bowl shattering and its echo reverberated throughout the house, louder than bones snapped out of place and blood gurgled into a milk-white abyss.

How others would die and seem so much more deserving of a better life, and she survived against her will only to continue this line of suffering. Eating a car crash explosion, getting fucked by it, giving birth to a curse, a dead name reborn, a ticking time bomb heart, a lone star over the bruised eyes, and a bullet hole between them. This world is a slaughterhouse, industrial capitalism, it is fucking itself into a lake of blood, like that which becomes a polluting sea in the city long after you'd leave it, but the prospect coexisted in the past. The back of your head was resting against the train tracks as you ate pounds of snow. Her body when it's found, his body in the daydream memory, six-inch-deep lacerations like tire tracks crunching through slush and snow on the rocky roads. Blood crusted up to turn black, the scorpion's heart, your seven sisters glow azure over their chests, guiding lights for one another, prismatic, in lime green ectoplasm, cartoony, an eternity.

As she crouched down with her paws shrouding her face, Rob held the night vision camera above and taped her distress. In the video, she radiated silver; her figure was a beaconing blur.

"I don't want to do this anymore," she pleaded to him, the recorder, and to G-d. "None of this is even worth it. It would be better for everyone if I could end it now."

When Rob closed his eyes, he imagined opening the passenger seat of the burning car, driving off to Texas with his dead best friend, and there was no pacemaker and alcoholic father. There was no corpse mutilated on the gravel road. Instead, there were the two of them at the Cowboys stadium, drinking piss beer, both of them with their own families and homes and careers, the skyline glowing pickle green from the outline of the Bank of America Plaza and the sphere on top of the Reunion Tower scintillating a light like that of a child's first vision after birth. And the distorted thought blurted out from him, "You're not the only one that's lost somebody. And to think you'd be so fucking willing to do that to me when you know how much I love you. Don't you think you survived for a reason? Even though I believe in nothing, and I'm not even sure if this reality is as fake as the distortion on the damaged tape in this camera, I have to believe surviving must be worth it. There's so much more beauty that we can't perceive yet. We just have to look beyond this cave, this hole carved inside us."

She disputed, dragging sweaty paws over her muzzle, smearing snot bubbles, "Nobody, not one creature, knows why it lives."

Lily petals rained upon them. It reminded her of what she saw when she last looked down from the school's rooftop. Somewhere else, you must have been rubbing those flowers between your thumb and index finger, and it was causing a storm like any other. How long had this been going on? Since your family had moved to Iowa? Before the Holocaust? It is all the same moment in one dying flower.

By custom, your sister had been buried less than a day after she killed herself. That same month, Efa had also died in a way that others deemed more natural and acceptable since she was debilitated with Down syn-

-drome and cerebral palsy. 'It must have been a relief for everyone,' you judged.

There were other tombstones in the cemetery with names yet to be inscribed on them, but you already knew who they were for. At the far-right end, near the pointed black fences and the green ash tree, there was a feral cub crouched beside a freshly dug grave, the dirt still damp and the grass tall around it. The boy was half wolf and half fox, an alien amalgamation of ebony and maroon. You knelt down beside him, took his hands from the urn that he had been squeezing like a lifeline, and took him into your chest.

"It's hard, I know," you pleaded to the child. "But you have to believe that he would want you to keep living and find happiness. And it's not fair at all. What happened wasn't a tragedy. Not to him, you, or anyone else buried here. None of it should have ever happened. Yet, we accept it, still burdened by the grief in every breath until our last words leave our lips, doing our best to achieve tikkun olam. You have no idea how much he will always love you, no matter what."

And the boy was wearing the yarmulke and tefillin and tallit that you had buried there months ago. You helped him bury the urn close to the grave and then, with muddy hands, took him to the end of the cemetery, where the crescent hills of golden corn and wet grass glimmered in the sunlight. When you turned to pull him closer into an embrace, you choked back tears and despair, seeing that he had disappeared into thin air, into stardust.

Sarah had taken Rob's hand as they silently walked across Saturn's rings. The lilies had stuck to their fur.

Even though his heart continued to tick, and outside of the fantasy, she was a homeless seventeen-year-old girl living inside a car outside of the small diner she was working at, she went on to disregard her tears and kissed him anyway.

It was around midnight when the phone downstairs started ringing, and then Riley's father began screaming out his name, telling him to pick up the phone while damning G-d in the same sentence. Heaven damned in Iowa buried in infernal cosmic snow. He let the phone ring for a while, unable to let go of the many thoughts and fantasies plaguing his mind. It was just a dream; the cub he'd been babysitting wasn't on the left side of his bed. It felt like pulling a lever when he lifted the phone.

There was the sobbing and sucking back snot before your voice spoke his name. His fur coat was a blanket of static beginning to spark. He thought he'd ignite into a torch at that very moment. Images of death were flashing behind his eyelids like a zoetrope.

Your sister was dead and had to be buried by the end of the next day. Mom and dad were too busy making arrangements with a Rabbi, making phone calls, screaming, breaking things, and collapsing. You asked if he could come over and pick you up, something, anything, to feel less alone. Confusion, shock, disillusionment, a slur of words, a vampiric wolf's tongue caught eating itself. He rambled nonsensically over your grief, "If you could see the film behind my eyelids right now, you wouldn't be calling me. The mov-

-ie... it's almost over. I can see the curtains closing. My movie."

A ruthless euphoria had begun to devastate him as Riley went on and dismissed the distorted sounds of fingers and snot sucked back up over the phone. "Ask me about the movie. What's the movie like, Riley? What's it about? Say it just like that. There's this kid, and I get this urge to hurt him. I've been holding the feeling in for a while after having so many opportunities in the past, and he's so young that I know what I say, the things I do, would permanently ruin him. I know I don't have a future. No ambitions, no hope. And I've never been happy in my entire life. Not even when I'm with you. I bet you thought differently, though. So, I'm sitting beside this kid in his Crayola red racecar bed, and I'm not a wolf anymore, my body is a nest of festering scorpions, and I put a hand on his shoulder. You see, Noah? I'm fucked. I'm so... fucking. FUCKED! It's getting worse. This is terminal. How much longer can I hold myself back from doing the worst thing ever? Do you still want me to come over?"

You couldn't comprehend a word he said, but you continued to beg until he went quiet for eons, stardust galaxy torn apart by the birth of a new black hole, titan rising, craters in the moon, and then he finally muddled out, "I'm coming over" before he hung up.

What the movie was like.

The synagogue was built with red brick and shaped like a perfect cube. One could only know it as a temple by the Star of David above the triad of arched glass windows. Decades ago, back when it was an Orthodox sanctuary, a staircase would lead to the women's gallery, which had now been converted into a kitchen. That is where everyone else had gathered while you stood between two sets of pews, staring at the Torah ark. The dust was sifting in the thick dewy air, the mold in the ceiling, and the last remnants of yesterday's torrential storm coating your fur. It was the hairpins that felt cursed in how they wouldn't hold your yarmulke still and the texture of the Israeli flags beside the half-filled bookcases. In knowing that this building would soon be empty, that most of the people upstairs wouldn't be living here in twenty years, that this town would be flooded with the blood of swine and bombed with methamphetamine. It was the white lilacs under your snout that smelled like a freshly cleaned baby blanket. And to think that Riley would be there, so different than how he was the day before, that he had pecked the back of your head, rubbed one finger over your collar, and guided you into his chest.

Broken ribs and vertebrae. Five feet of snow piled up by the front door. Blinded and still driving. Two towns over and where Rob lived, the breadth of forest green hills among thousands of acres of farmland, a place one could go back to in a century, and everything would still be the same, for better and worse. Incessant even in the face of EF3 tornadoes. Another harvest season, another grating winter, yet the emerald glint of the red cedar trees would continue to flourish.

A tree is planted in the front yard of Sarah's house. It is the forgiveness and open arms of two parents, then folding in on themselves. Maybe they will open again someday. There is flesh in the dirt, hope in her heart, and a quilt from grandma over your shoulder. A wheelchair that once belonged to Efa, next to the wooden gazebo, always repositioned to face away from the sun.

Death, the heaviest matter in the universe. Not skeletal, but a supreme cloak that shrouds the heart, replacing the hope with helplessness. Death hides somewhere in a gothic tomb in a monolithic graveyard near your grandmother's house, where she often goes for eight-mile runs in the morning. And yet, there is his tree, a few feet taller each year, the branches still healthy and swaying in the autumn wind as treefrogs and cicadas sing from one rural town to the other. It's in your breath.

Who's that kid sitting alone in the theater?

The movie is over.

Not long after your sister and Efa's death, your parents confronted you, right as you had come through the door with the accordion after stretching each note as long as possible in dedication to the night and the dead. Mom said, "Come here," and then, "Come here, Noah." That aggressive bark in her spiteful throat. You couldn't recall if she had ever said she loved you before.

"What's been going on with you and that older boy from Parker County," Dad besieged. "Got something you want to confess? Put the fucking instrument down and come to the fucking table."

You gawked and staggered, squeezing the sides of your denim overalls, and stood over one of the chairs before you awkwardly explained, "I work at his parent's dairy farm. You know that. I help with painting, cleaning, mowing, and just about everything. Not sure what's the big deal about that. What's wrong with Riley?"

Dad threw a metal strainer filled with lettuce at your chest. The punch to the gut. Out of breath. You closed your eyes and could see the rest of the movie.

"That kid is a queer, Noah," Dad spoke loud and unafraid. "Just like you. It's true, ain't it? Everyone knows it. That kid is a faggot. These are small towns. Everyone knows everyone's business. Don't you know? I don't get what's up with you fucking kids anymore. A fucking faggot for a son. And your cousin, that whore."

Since mother was crying, he had to narrate her emotions, "You see what your mother is going through?

She's had to bury every one of her kids now. Because you're as good as dead to her. Now get your things, go to Grandma's, and knock on her door. I'm sure she believes G-d can save a sinner like you. Dumb as bricks. But we're not gonna be your parents anymore. You fuckin' listening? Get going, faggot!"

Brice's pointer finger to your chest and into a fist to your stomach, out of breath, the GAP hoodie, gay and proud. You stood tall and strong, not just for yourself, but for him, a vampire you didn't even know. Tears, they'd flow, your tail swiftly whipped like a pendulum. Him just yelling get going faggot you hear me, faggot, queer, homo, homosexual, his spit over your face. He pushed you once by the shoulders, and you pushed him just as hard, thrusting him against the table, and then canine teeth slobbered as you growled viciously back at him. The table collapsed, and then the two of you were on top of it, mother in the corner. She was still holding a mess of crochet threads in her hands, your claws digging at his throat, his bandaged hands beating at your head. Once he pushed you over, you taunted your mother, punched her shoulders like drums, and screamed, "Which womb did the faggot come from? Whose sperm made this homo that you call your son? You hate me? I hate you all just as much! Why couldn't you protect us? You killed my sister! Why didn't you fucking help her? Yeah, I'm gay. I'm gay and proud! Fuck you all!"

Dad had the shotgun to the back of your head, and you could feel its weight and power before it bashed you into the collapsed table. His words from before went on like a broken record, shattering whatever pride you had. He shot the accordion first and then followed behind as you crawled back out the front door, never to return or see their faces again.

This part was meant to be one of the first scenes in the movie. Here, it's been edited a bit, reconstructed, with different characters, in a separate storyline, but it seems better fitting here. The dialogue cannot be presented as fact but only as symbolic interpretation and gross imaginations of actual events. You're in Riley's bed, and he's sitting on the side with one hand gliding up your back and shirt.

Action.

"You can't stay here forever," he murmured.

The stroke of his hand made you momentarily displace the grief and the terrifying visuals of your sister's corpse. Maybe he loved you. No, you were sure of it, no matter what happened in his brain or whatever corrupted his soul. What is corrupted? Could it still show affection? If it would hurt, if it could twist, crunch, bruise, and destroy a world, could it still, somehow, have the ability to be gentle and true? It is the cancer, the slow rot inside, which you could never comprehend, not even now. That it could infect and infest and plague.

It had taken almost a week for you to remember the phone call. You turned over and smirked playfully, having not sensed what was making him sweat, and asked, "What did you mean when you said if I could see the film... behind your eyes? What could you see?"

He smirked, almost as if it were all a joke. You in his bed. Your sister's death. How fucked it was that you had to live with your grandma and cousin until your relatives up north could take you. And then you'd live with an Orthodox family, destined to help manage a kosher slaughterhouse. Whatever this was, it would then be bisected. There were other things, too, like the boy he would babysit, his father beating and raping his mom, the car on fire, too many things. What he wanted to do was, maybe, put his hand over your mouth, pull down your pants, and rape you, but he hadn't become that yet. Instead, he pretended that you said nothing and turned on the radio.

It is the sound of the mournful clean electric guitar at the beginning of the Aerosmith 'Dream On' song continuously playing in the cathedral as families and cubs walk around the jet-black coffin inside the Catholic cathedral. And it's raining because it always is when the distorted static of a song played on cheap speakers ends up being as haunting as the song itself. Somewhere else, another boy is listening along on top of a beanbag with his temporary brother. It's a different song, but the feeling is the same. Mortality of shattered youth. Childhood without nostalgia. The playground flooded. Dead body in the woods, along the pavement, over the backyard grass, in a frigid hospital bed, outside the front yard, and the ghosts you met along the way.

Riley snapped the clips that had come undone so that your yarmulke stayed on your head, which caused your ears to twitch while you dreamed of the wolf-fox boy. He apologized and decided to go downstairs and sleep on the sofa. In a better world, his apology would have ended his disease, and none of this would have ever existed.

The tough sinew in the tree's branches outside of Sarah's house still swaying, forever.

One night later, you fell asleep outside the Jewish cemetery and dreamed of the Ku Klux Klan burning down the temple. You were only a baby when they protested in white gowns near your house of worship. Had they come from hundreds of miles away, traveling from one town and to the next, or could they have been your neighbors? They could go ahead and torch it. What did it matter to you? In a few years, it would be transformed into a Baptist church, anyway.

A white dove pecking at your ears startled you awake. You snarled and chomped your muzzle at it, only wanting to scare it, not eat it, and growled, "Dammit, I'll crush you in one bite! Back off!"

The bird fluttered its wings upon a grave that had too much lichen on it to reveal a name. White wings, like the first snowfall in November. It danced back up above your head and slowly flew toward the rusted gates. Beyond them was Grandma's house, a door you were afraid to knock, and the synagogue. You sniffed the dead leaves that mimicked the color of your fur and crunched branches as you suspiciously followed the bird. It guided you into the temple, where the door was ajar, and the only light inside came from the lamp above the ark.

As the doors behind you slowly shut, you hesitated and came to a halt, shifting your head to both sides of the pews. The dove had transformed mid-air into a beaming orb. Dozens more orbs drifted from the ceiling and to the seats. Your breath emitted cold vapor as the temple became frigid, even as the lights became brighter, and the lamp by the ark sizzled. The lights took form, standing and sitting, foxes, deer, dressed in suits, some wearing tzitzit, others veiling their heads and torso in prayer shawls.

You saw your brother and sister in a trance, davening, and had not noticed as you stepped up to stand beside them. They seemed so real, and yet none of it could have been. Everyone here was dead. As they prayed, they emitted no sound. Not even your paws made the typical creaks on the worn-out floorboards.

As the tears came and blinded your eyes, you heard your older brother whisper, "Even though none of us are on this plane anymore, we still come here to pray. To bless these towns even as they're torn asunder. Even after every last fox and deer in our community has moved away or passed on. This is the closest we can get to you. You'll think this was only a dream when you wake up, but I promise it's not. Some people are only given this gift once or twice. Others might never receive it. Even then, people disregard it... I pray that you keep hope, even though I'm gone because I know you'd want me to do the same if situations were reversed. The next time you see me, it'll be here, the cemetery, or maybe even along the soybean fields, and I'll teach you how we pray and bless others."

How is it that Grandmother always seemed to be in such a harmonious bliss as someone would feel after accepting the inevitability of their death and the glory of being fucked by a cosmic halo? It made no sense that this woman would exist, sitting on her lavender sofa, writing poetry, and putting together family pho-tobooks. You knew nobody as religious as her, so devoted to an endless prayer, a conversation with a G-d that likely never cared. Born in a Holocaust. Raised in corrosive abuse. Beaten and raped. Children she gave birth to, some already gone as nothing more than tiny rotting skeletons.

An aurora was visible outside the open window and dusty curtains and mirrored the gash above your right eye. As you held a wet towel to the wound, you asked her fearfully, expecting vengeful judgment, "How do you go on after everything you've been through? Because I don't know if I can do it. What my sister did… Maybe I should have leaped as well, after I had found her."

The silence was thick and humid as an electric mist shrouded all of western Iowa. A coyote from a few houses down yipped and howled to the sound of cars speeding by on the unpaved roads. She exclaimed faintly, creepingly, "I had thought about my death many times when your grandfather was beating me. Once, I had left my children in the hands of others so that I could seek shelter until he'd gone completely mad and left this world. Then I had the shame and weight of so much on my shoulders. So much death, always. I imagine you can hear the train tracks quite well outside your window.

Even though they're too far from me, I hear them too, along with the sound of ocean waves. I hear the sound of Efa sobbing after I gave birth to her. Losing so many, I could see it as meaningless; that's how your youthful mind imagines death. Instead, I have learned to cherish those faint smiles I captured and shared with those I loved and aren't with me physically any-more. Your soul will grow stronger."

"But I don't want it to grow stronger like that," you argued. "What does it matter when their deaths were so meaningless, horrifying, and haunted with the most extreme pains? I'd take my life and prefer whatever comes after, even if it's an abyss."

Grandmother rebutted, "When you're born, the first thing you see is a light, and they say that when you die, the last thing you see is the same light. What if you took your life and woke up to choose between that decision again? You have to keep trying, Noah. Don't you think G-d would prefer if you continued to use your pain to help others? At the least, G-d gives you the earth to find endless gratefulness. There will always be more to you than this hurt."

Your cousin was wearing an oversized Metallica con-cert t-Shirt and a miniskirt when she passed you by in the kitchen and began to clean Grandma's dishes that filled the sink. The sun beamed across her thick blonde hair that had been held back in a ponytail, which was cut halfway down from her tail. While she worked and went to school, you waited to be taken away by distant relatives, watched TV with Grannie, prayed along without knowing what the Hebrew meant, combed her hair, painted her nails, listened to records and tapes with Sarah, cried at any point that you saw yourself in a mirror or when it was too si-lent, but mostly fantasized of living in that little farm-house forever. 'This must be what heaven is like,' you thought. How far would you have to keep walking in the cornfields until you'd find your deceased siblings? Would they join you? Does the pain end after death and once you finally get a taste of Heaven?

The two of you went outside and sat in a tractor together, thinking fuck it, rejection is freedom. There could be nothing better than being told to leave a place you believed was an inescapable prison. Sarah held a wooden jewelry box in both hands and wondered whether she should bury it here or hold onto it forever. A gift could feel like a curse, but the sentimental value might have just as much power.

"I'm pregnant." She smiled and looked away from you as she went on with silence between her words. "And I'm gonna keep it. Family hates me enough for this. If I had an abortion... It's too expensive and too far away. Plus. I have something to live for now. I can't kill myself if I'm a mother: Rob and I. You know him. The Ark's. We have a plan. We'll find a way to move to Texas as soon as I graduate. We'll go to school, get a house, eight-hundred and sixty miles from here, we'll raise this kid to be the biggest Cowboys fan, he will play football and baseball, we'll make him wear cowboy hats, and I'll dress in all black, be his hippie goth mom, and he's going to have the happiest life. There's hope for us. I believe in it."

You sat there in silence as the dread became overwhelming. What she felt couldn't be relayed. The sunrise, that portrait of the rolling hills, the cool still air, it couldn't have felt any more deceptive.

"I'm gay."

"Yeah, I know. I've always known." She opened the jewelry box. Necklaces, chokers, bracelets, anklets, all tangled in knots.

"For how long?"

"As long as I can remember," she confessed. "Just. I knew you were different in a certain way. I'm different, too. I don't know how to say it. You don't realize that you're as brave as I am. That's why... It's hard to imagine, but I think you'd make a good father someday, maybe in a time, place, and world where you're not hated for simply existing. I have faith that it'll come."

She found the most stereotypically queer bracelet that she could find and put it in your left palm. Even if there weren't any hope, this glimmer of light would be enough until the curtains closed.

You stared at her stomach, imagined the child inside, who your cousin stated was already assigned as a male, and questioned her, "What if he turns out to be like me? Then what?"

One claw traced along the wooden case inside of the open jewelry box. A tattoo of her son's name is embedded across her heart. She mumbled with insecurity, "I do worry about Rob and what he would think. But he would come around if our son wasn't straight. I think I'd let our kid figure it out for himself, and I wouldn't pressure him to come out. But I'd want to give him enough signs to know that it would be okay to do it. Rob would come around. Someone he knows, who was involved in the car crash, they might come and live with us in Texas for a while, and everyone's pretty sure he's gay."

"Riley? He's going to live with you?"

"It could help. He's good with kids; he could watch over our son when we're in school or working. All we'd ask is for him to pay a small amount. I trust him." She smirked and saw the man who meant most to you in your eyes. "I think you should come to Texas, too. Maybe you could stay with us. You know that I'm never going to abandon you, right?"

"Right." The bracelet felt like a warm halo in your hands. "I don't believe in it yet, that concept of hope, but I'll keep trying." After you slipped it over your wrist, you collapsed onto her legs, stared at the gages and the tractor's steering wheel, and assured her, "You're going to be a great mother."

Sarah opened the jewelry box and rubbed a claw over the words written with a black sharpie, which read, **'I LOVE YOU, MOMMIE**.' And it made her sob with vicious hate that only a mother could understand. He didn't think he loved her anymore, but maybe in a decade or two, she would show him what he wrote in it, and he'd suddenly love her for at least trying as hard as she did.

You woke up crying again but couldn't recall a single fragment from the dream. It was the noxious scent of bacon frying in the kitchen, the landline phone ringing for the third time, your back sliding down the cabinets before you brought your kneecaps to your shoulders and the sound of aggressive banging near a dangling doorknob. Your soon-to-be ex-boyfriend brought you back to clarity when he tossed the bulky phone at your side and slammed the door. One more ring, and then you'd be done wiping up the snot and tears.

What had and hadn't changed in thirteen years since the two of you had left that decrepit vulture town flooded in gore from the illegally operated slaughterhouse. How you had given in and learned to love your lisp, that it projected a false optimism and separated you from those who'd rather hide in self-hate. It didn't matter if you never spoke to your parents again. Whatever farmland you would've inherited if you hadn't been queer, it didn't matter anymore since you could manage multiple stores while being out of the closet. But love still seemed like an impossible obstacle, plagued by those who wanted only heartless hookups or those who could only love by using coercion against someone younger than them. There would be no high school sweetheart like Sarah had been gifted. That wolf was long dead from a bullet to ash, anyway.

Riley's suicide, what it must have looked like, the end of the film, winding around your eyes as you picked up the phone. It was your cousin again. She was begging you to pick D up from daycare and give him a fun day, whatever that meant. Take him to the movies, to Dave and Buster's, just not the mall where he got molested or the other mall where you both worked and where the suicide happened. What did the last part matter? You knew how much he loved ice-skating. After giving in, you observed your partner from the living room corner as he ate silently in the kitchen. He hadn't known that tomorrow was meant to be your last day of work and that the day after, you'd pack all of your belongings into your daffodil-colored jeep and cruise away to Omaha, back to where Riley thought you'd best belong. It had to happen, even if it meant risking death.

There were things you knew you could never speak to the boy about, even if the vague reminder would always be indisputably present. He'd seen a piece in Riley that you never imagined could exist. You could feel the weight of his trauma in his emerald eyes, which also carried yours, his mothers, fathers, and so on throughout the mostly deceased ancestral line. Furthermore, you could sense that he was gay, something his parents hadn't uncovered yet, if they ever would. You'd want to tell him the red flags to look out for in the future, to not confuse love with someone else's obsession, not to hold firm that sex would liberate the inner scars, to come out early and love himself instead of spending years worrying what others might or might not think. To not make all of the mistakes you had made. And how sorry you were, as selfish as it would be to confess since there's no way you could've known or stopped any of it. What chance was there that D would ever come out on his own? His father had already despised you, and then after what Riley did...

When you made it to the daycare, D was in the arcade room, slamming buttons between two of his friends, wearing only his mint green swimming trunks. The fur along his back was glossy jet black, and then there were patches of cherry red that blended in along his stomach, chest, wrists, and legs. He was the only crossbreed in the room. One of the kids nabbed at him to get his attention until he twisted around and gawked in a jolt of enthusiasm. He sprinted forth, squeezed his arms around your waist, and you were sure you'd never seen a tail wag as fiercely as that cub. "Noah!" He shouted your name. "You're picking me up today? Yes! Yes yes yes yes yes! Can we get tacos and ice cream and go skating? Can you help me win a lava lamp?"

As the wolf-fox guided you down the halls and past the activity rooms, you concentrated on the black yarmulke that blended in with the fur between his ears. Maybe, there remained fragments of innocence hidden inside of him.

'It must be nice to have children,' you begrudged. You were sure that you could raise him better. In a different world with a distant future, you would become a father to children who had been damaged and give them the love that you weren't given back then. You would have an American dream like your cousins and make just as much money and be the one sending postcards of you with a better partner on holidays. Family members and friends would hang them up on their fridges instead of tossing them away because being queer would finally be accepted in even the most conservative states.

Once D was settled in the car, you saw a glint in his eyes, like an angel waking up for the first time in heaven from a long and harrowing slumber. You weren't the one he sought in heaven, but he was sure you could help guide him. When the engine started, he held tight to his seat belt, preparing for impact, even though the car had yet to take off. In his name, the sparks from an exploding car that could never be snuffed out—cursed, haunted. How could a body encapsulate so many deaths?

You took him to the mall and watched him ice skate across the exact spot where someone recently killed themselves. Instead of winning the lava lamp, the two of you exchanged tickets for loads of candy, a Dave and Buster's shirt, and a basketball. You took him for chocolate fudge ice cream, picked out candles that Sarah might like as a gift, and stopped by to say hello to the people at the Banana Republic clothing store where you worked and the Coach handbag store where his mother worked.

On the way home, you captured the childlike glee radiating from him. There wasn't any music on the radio, but his shoulders shifted from side to side, his chin bounced in waves, and his fingers tapped at his knees. You imagined his excitement would have caused an accident if his tail were longer. His mom would swear that his brain was mostly a cancer of constant fear and psychotic rage from the ruthless trauma, but here he was, in a euphoric bliss over some hidden song and vision.

Another car swerved into your lane, and you slammed on the brakes with little time to react. Your brawny yellow jeep sped off the road into a field of unkempt grass as tall as the wheels. Your right hand was on the wheel while the left was in front of the boy's chest. As soon as you realized you were both alive, you begged him not to tell his mother, especially about the curse words that naturally slipped out of your mouth. However, he hadn't responded, so you gazed at him and saw him paralyzed like a terrifying sculpture. The vision he once had was suddenly replaced, and you immediately felt it as if it were an extension of yourself. In his eyes were the silver steel frames bent and twisting into flesh, the spark of a matchstick ex-

-ploding into a fireball of corpses, your brother and T, connected by death, bodies falling from rooftops and out of windows, gunpowder and vomit, the last kiss you shared with Riley, and then him holding the boy down, giving him carpet burns as he thrust into D, his arm digging into his back, blood pouring from the cub's busted nostrils, and then brain matter spattered on concrete and leaking into artificial grass.

One reel of film reached its end, and another clicked and spun.

And then you were gone.

The end of the film as envisioned behind D's eyes.

A shadow was hunched over and slowly moving toward him on the other side of the dimly lit hallway. Even though the hall was twelve feet long, it felt like they were half a mile apart. Behind the figure was a door leading to where the dance music had been coming from, and he was determined to make it through. The boy's teeth protruded from his muzzle as slobber coated his neck and poured onto the floor. It wasn't intimidated; the figure continued to drag forward. He struck down with one paw, hoping to mark his territory, gritted his teeth so hard it ached, and gnarled under his breath.

Painful groans echoed down the hall, making him fear that it might be better to flee than attack. He thought it could have been Bloody Mary. As it came closer, he could make out the details of a feathery ashen gray dress painted with streaks of blood. The body seemed frail and defeated, moving as if hoping to collapse into his embrace. He thought that maybe it wanted to be cannibalized. Its face, once distorted and absent of direction, suddenly grinned wickedly. What had once moved at a snail's pace raced faster and fell over him. His teeth clenched down and tore out panels from the floor. When he let go of the figure, his mother took its form. She brushed the fur around his neck, rubbed the necklace hanging from it, and soothed his rage as tears wallowed her face.

The dance floor was vacant except for a single soul dressed in a fern green suit jacket, brown corduroy pants, black dress shoes, a floral button-up shirt, and a tie designed with koi fish. D imagined himself out of place, seeing that he had nothing on, having woken up from the sound of uplifting trance blaring outside his bedroom and felt driven as if it were his destiny to find this room. This unreality had become just as real and vital for him to continue existing. He needed it to be real, if not now, at least as a fragmentary heaven of gray matter or at the center of the cobweb.

A tall and hefty bear held out one paw and tried to hold back his tears. The boy took it carefully, unsure where he was now and in awe that their love had lived long enough to transcend and become this space. There was no Texas anymore. Concepts of identity had no meaning.

"My precious cub," the bear cried gaily. "You waited, and you came for me. But it wasn't supposed to be like this. I'm so… so sorry."

They held tight to one another, imagining that if they let go, they'd be apart in different realities again. It wouldn't be like that anymore, but the fear was difficult to endure. Time was nonexistent, the song would repeat forever, and it didn't matter if they slow danced for what might feel like a few more hours. They'd have the rest of eternity to swing freely in front of the hissing smoke machine, disco ball, and kaleidoscopic strobe light.

Orbs casually drifted in the soft moonlight and poured through glass rooftops. They hid behind the boy and silently swayed into his manifold of a coat. D stood in the food court of the massive mall, feeling as if it were his own castle. He felt the silver handrails and gazed down at the ice rink, looked left to the Barnes & Noble, and then stood in front of the Build-a-Bear store, imagining a teddy bear in his arms, but supersized, quadruple the size of himself, and unable to be pulled apart, the fluffy cotton inside of it as tough as diamonds.

There would always be an arcade room with the backdoor open, indecipherable voices from the waterpark mumbling in the distance while the sky twisted its ribs into chrome, and a mile-long playground with a scorching hot tar floor. If he shut his eyes and focused long enough, he could sometimes enter these liminal spaces again, but each time he felt he was on the verge of fully returning, it was if he were in time-out again. Time-out for eons. However, he allowed himself to venture back to the vacant daycare playgrounds, in a world where there was only him and ghosts left behind.

D lifted himself by a miniature fire pole and climbed onto a slide. The moon was hidden, unveiling an ocean of scintillating stars over the daycare center. One paw traced constellations from Leo to Gemini, and he whispered, "I see you all. I see my births. I see the ether. I'll make this my truth, a childhood that can be eternal."

He twirled around on the slide and faced the soccer field, which had been overrun with prickly weeds. There, in the far corner, that's where he and four other boys had once formed a circle and compared dicks. As he sucked on his spit with the air flowing between his teeth, he could feel that moment rush through him again.

Ghosts guided him as he slid down and walked from the asphalt of the playground and through muddy blades of grass. He tracked to the side of the gated building, where the bathrooms were hidden. As he stood still, he took a whiff of the air and inhaled the hot fragrance of semen, iron, and sweat. It could have been another boy, man, or even Bloody Mary, hidden and patiently waiting inside for him. It could have even been the long-lost and dead love of his life. Or it could have been like in The Goonies when the wrong note of the skeleton keys could drop someone into a pit of death. Any possibility would suffice him.

He opened the door, which had seemed empty at first, but upon a second glance, he noticed a single pair of cartoon briefs behind the toilet. Water dripped and echoed from the sink as he tried to recall a blurry memory. The rainbow friendship bracelet he gave Evan was on his wrist now, he was wearing the Danny Phantom costume his parents bought him from eBay for Halloween, and a mossy green rock dangled from his neck and down to the bottom of his ribcage. As he carefully kneeled and went to pick up the pair of briefs, the door slowly shut upon him and locked with a caustic bang. The wolf fox hid under the leaking sink and his ears twitched to the sound of each momentary drop of water. A twisted urge poisoned his thoughts, which he knew were all he had left. At any moment, it could happen; a perverted light would overtake and desecrate him until he'd become like the other ghostly orbs spliced and caught under each strand of his hair. Without remorse, he pressed the piss-stained underwear to his face, sucked in deeply, and let out a passive moan as he gripped his cock.

X   X   X

THE
END

ACKNOWLEDGMENTS

Thank you, Evan Femino, for not only publishing this book but for being my friend as well. Thank you, Neptune, for being the first person to read this book and being a wonderful, beautiful person and musician. Thanks to all my friends throughout writing this, especially Zenny, Keyboard, and Teddy. Big thanks to Dennis Cooper for always supporting other outsider writers like me. Thank you, David, for always inspiring me with your art, being my friend throughout the years, and the photography used for this book. Thanks to Axel (@ddumyyy) for the beautiful art piece used for the final chapter. Thank you, to the person reading this, for your support. Thank you, Jon; even though you're not with me in person, I know you're still close to me in other ways. I love you, always and forever.

Front and back cover photo by David Agasi
You can find more of his art at davidagasi.com

Art piece for An Iowa Tail by Axel/ddumyyy
You can find more of their art at
Twitter.com/ddumyyy

Damien Ark
photographed by David Agasi in San Francisco, CA

FERAL DOVE

FERAL DOVE
BOOKS

© Damien Ark 2023

ISBN 979-8-9856764-5-7

Thank you for being here.

Cover & interior book design by Evan Femino

www.feraldove.com

Printed in the USA
CPSIA information can be obtained
at www.ICGtesting.com
LVHW091505271023
762201LV00012B/1564